**PENGUIN
SPECIALS**

Penguin Specials fill a gap. Written by some of today's most exciting and insightful writers, they are short enough to be read in a single sitting – when you're stuck on a train; in your lunch hour; between dinner and bedtime. Specials can provide a thought-provoking opinion, a primer to bring you up to date, or a striking piece of fiction. They are concise, original and affordable.

To browse digital and print Penguin Specials titles, please refer to **penguin.com.au/penguinspecials**

LOWY INSTITUTE

The Lowy Institute is an independent, nonpartisan international policy think tank. The Institute provides high-quality research and distinctive perspectives on the issues and trends shaping Australia's role in the world. The Lowy Institute Papers are peer-reviewed essays and research papers on key international issues affecting Australia and the world.

For a discussion on *Man of Contradictions* with Ben Bland and leading Indonesia experts, visit the Lowy Institute's daily commentary and analysis site, *The Interpreter*: **lowyinstitute.org/the-interpreter/debate/man-of-contradictions**

Ben Bland is Director of the Southeast Asia Program at the Lowy Institute. Ben was previously an award-winning correspondent for the *Financial Times* in Indonesia, China, and Vietnam. His first book, *Generation HK: Seeking Identity in China's Shadow*, was acclaimed as a 'prescient, rollicking read' by the *Financial Times*, a 'David versus Goliath tale' by the *Sydney Morning Herald*, and 'lively' and 'illuminating' by the *Times Literary Supplement*.

LOWY INSTITUTE

Man of Contradictions

A LOWY INSTITUTE PAPER

BY BEN BLAND

PENGUIN BOOKS

UK | USA | Canada| Ireland | Australia
India | New Zealand | South Africa | China

Penguin Books is part of the Penguin Random House group of companies
whose addresses can be found at global.penguinrandomhouse.com.

Penguin
Random House
Australia

First published by Penguin Books, 2020

Cover image by Money Sharma/Getty Images

Typeset by Midland Typesetters, Australia

Printed and bound in Australia by Griffin Press, part of Ovato, an accredited
ISO AS/NZS 14001 Environmental Management Systems printer

A catalogue record for this
book is available from the
National Library of Australia

ISBN 978 1 76089 724 6

penguin.com.au

'The most obvious sign of the man of Power is, quite consistently, his ability . . . to absorb Power from the outside, and to concentrate within himself apparently antagonistic opposites.'
Benedict Anderson, *Language and Power: Exploring Political Cultures in Indonesia*

'Do I contradict myself?
Very well then I contradict myself,
(I am large, I contain multitudes.)'
Walt Whitman, *Song of Myself*

'A foolish consistency is the hobgoblin of little minds . . . To be great is to be misunderstood.'
Ralph Waldo Emerson, *Self-Reliance*

CONTENTS

Introduction

Indonesia is the best country in the world in which to be a foreign correspondent. There are many reasons why: the wealth of stories, the warmth of the people, the ease of access to political leaders, and the sheer size and diversity of the nation. There is no other place you can see, learn, and do so much as a journalist while feeling so secure, at least most of the time. But, truth be told, I was anxious in the early months after I arrived in Jakarta in 2012, having moved from a posting for the *Financial Times* in Hanoi.

Uprooting your life and starting over again is hard enough anywhere. Getting your head around Indonesia, a nation that charms, confuses, and confounds in equal measure is another challenge altogether. So, I was lucky to be thrust, early on, into covering what turned out to be a defining election campaign.

The 2012 race to be governor of Jakarta was my introduction to the rambunctious world of Indonesian democracy – bitterly fought, enlivened by popular enthusiasm, tinged by corruption, but ultimately based on free and fair elections. It brought me face-to-face with the personalities and problems that would define this country for a decade. And it prompted me eventually to write this book.

Joko Widodo was the underdog challenger for the Jakarta governorship. He was taking on an establishment candidate who was backed by the president and a host of well-connected politicians and businesspeople. The former furniture manufacturer, who grew up in a riverside shack, had become a national political sensation as mayor of Solo, his home city in Central Java.[1]

In the early years of Indonesia's second experiment with democracy, Jokowi, as he is known, had shown a new way of doing things – listening to people, fixing broken markets, building new homes for slum dwellers, and setting a rare example of corruption-free leadership. He had an unmatched instinct for retail politics and was able to electrify an election campaign without saying much. His rivals had to hand out envelopes of cash in a forlorn attempt to catch up.[2]

After he won the first round of the election in July 2012, I went to his campaign headquarters in the hope of grabbing a quick word. The house in the leafy suburb of Menteng was throbbing with jubilant supporters and excitable journalists who mobbed him as he entered. I somehow managed to dart between the closing ranks of sweaty bodies and sat down next to Jokowi. 'What impact will your victory have on Indonesia?' I blurted out.

Jokowi turned to me, bemused, and answered in the Javanese-accented English that would later become familiar to world leaders and global business executives. He believed that his victory would prove to all Indonesians that 'not only money' wins votes, 'but also the heart and the head'.[3] It wasn't much of an exclusive. But the pace of the campaign had hooked me on Indonesia and this unique character, who would dominate the country's politics for the next decade.

I would go on to meet or interview Jokowi more than a dozen times as he rose from mayor of Solo to governor of Jakarta, and then president of a nation of more than 270 million people.[4] As a journalist, and then later as a foreign policy analyst, I would watch the Jokowi phenomenon grow exponentially before crumbling under the burden of expectations. Through his campaign promises and his own back-story, Jokowi embodied long-thwarted hopes for a better Indonesia – a country with faster economic growth, lower rates of poverty, more jobs, less corruption, and a political system that served the people, not the powerful.

By 'struggling alone', as one adviser phrased it, Jokowi would finally tame the 'octopus of oligarchy' that had been holding back Indonesia since the Suharto era, devouring its natural resources, corrupting its bureaucracy, and defrauding its people.[5] Jokowi's new Indonesia would be a strong, successful country that made its citizens proud and its neighbours envious, attracting long queues of foreign investors keen to capitalise on its rise.

The president doubled down on this vision in his second inauguration speech after his re-election in 2019. His ambition was for Indonesia to become a developed nation by 2045, and one of the world's five biggest economies, up from its current sixteenth place.[6] With a reformed bureaucracy and an open, competitive economy, this Indonesia would have 'social justice for all' and per capita incomes similar to Portugal or Taiwan today.

Many outsiders have been captivated by Jokowi and his towering aspirations for Indonesia. Singapore's *The Straits Times* named him 'Asian of the Year' in 2019 because of his 'ability to foster unity in an age of chaos and disruption'.[7] Malcolm

Turnbull, the former Australian prime minister who became friendly with Jokowi while in office, called him 'one of the most important leaders in the world' and 'a cool cat in every respect'.[8]

Upon closer examination, however, the longer Jokowi spent in the presidential palace, the more his promise faded. By his second term, the man who pitched himself as an outsider had become deeply embedded in elite politics. A leader once admired for his clean reputation had weakened the nation's highly popular anti-corruption agency, prompting an outbreak of student protests. And his persistent calls for economic transformation had been hamstrung by a lack of focus.

The cracks in his leadership have been exposed by the COVID-19 crisis.[9] Rather than rising to the challenge, like some other leaders, Jokowi has struggled under the immense pressure. He initially withheld information about the extent of the pandemic, saying he did not want to panic the public. As the death toll rose, he vacillated between taking the necessary mitigation measures and suggesting there was little to worry about.

His government demonstrated many of its worst traits: a disregard for expert advice, a lack of trust in civil society, and a failure to develop a coherent strategy. While showing the weaknesses of the health system, the COVID-19 pandemic has also set back Jokowi's economic plans, halting growth, making two million unemployed, and wiping out a decade of progress in curbing poverty.[10]

Jokowi's most jaded former followers see a man who has fallen from grace and sold out the promise of reform. But I see a more complicated picture. The higher he has risen, the more Jokowi's contradictions have revealed themselves – and the more he seems trapped by the contradictions of Indonesia's turbulent history, 75 years after declaring independence from the Netherlands.

If you ask Jokowi about politics, he will tell you it is blindingly obvious. You just ask the people what they want, then go and do it. Check that bureaucrats are doing their job and not stealing money, and corruption will be resolved, while investment and economic growth will soar.

But despite his disarmingly straightforward dictums, Jokowi remains an enigmatic figure. He has consistently surprised his sternest critics and disappointed his strongest supporters. After winning the presidency in 2014, he was resoundingly re-elected in 2019. However, he has struggled to turn success at the ballot box into the transformational change Indonesia desperately needs if it is to ensure a better future for its citizens.

The president is caught between the promise of democracy and the deep roots of authoritarianism in Indonesia. Jokowi has made economic growth the centrepiece of his administration. But he has been unable to square the desperate need for foreign investment with a culture of protectionism and scepticism towards economic liberalisation. He has attempted to advocate for religious tolerance and diversity. But he has ended up co-opting, or being co-opted by, the forces of conservative Islam.

Jokowi's leadership style is paradoxical. He presents himself as a master of micromanagement, one whose mantra is 'go to the ground' and 'check, check, check'.[11] Yet he often makes policy on the hoof, without any solid analytical basis, from his response to the COVID-19 crisis, to his plans for a new capital city in the jungles of Kalimantan. He has rarely shown much outward ambition or interest in politics. Yet, his inner drive has pushed him to grasp the top job from the hands of the nation's wealthiest, greediest, and most corrupt politicians. Inspired but exasperated by Jokowi, one of his ministers told me that it was best to understand the president as a 'bundle of contradictions'.

This book is my attempt to elucidate some of these contradictions. I've spent nearly 20 years trying to make sense of this country, first as a student of

Indonesian politics, then as a foreign correspondent and, now, as an analyst. For the past eight years, I've been gripped by the rise and travails of Jokowi. In addition to my interactions with the president, I've interviewed dozens of his ministers, senior officials, financial backers, and assorted hangers-on to learn what makes him tick.

Whenever I could, I tried to get out of Jakarta to listen to the ordinary people whose ambitions Jokowi tries to reflect. I travelled tens of thousands of kilometres across this vast archipelago by aircraft, car, ferry, canoe, trishaw, and horse-and-cart. From black magicians and former terrorists, to illegal gold miners and satay sellers, I'm grateful that the many Indonesians I have met have (almost) always welcomed my prying questions.

This book is the first English language political biography of Jokowi. But it is not a conventional biography. While I hope I have portrayed Jokowi fairly, I could not possibly tell his whole life story in such a short work. Instead, I want to use the incredible tale of the small-town furniture maker turned world leader to shed some light on the story of Indonesia.

I believe that a man who rose to power by tapping into the hopes and dreams of tens of millions of Indonesians embodies the contradictions of these people and this nation. It is only by understanding his contradictions that we can fully understand where he and his country are heading.

CHAPTER ONE

The furniture maker who captured a nation's imagination

Early in Jokowi's presidency, China's assertive behaviour in the South China Sea presented him with one of his first major foreign policy challenges. Beijing was inflaming tensions by building artificial islands and military installations in waters claimed by several of Indonesia's Southeast Asian neighbours. Although Indonesia was not directly involved, some of Jokowi's top diplomats wanted him to push back against China by making a strong public statement in defence of international law and freedom of navigation. They believed Indonesia should act as a mediating power in Southeast Asia, alleviating the growing regional frictions with China.

But Jokowi was struggling to comprehend the relevance of events beyond Indonesia's own waters. Why spend valuable diplomatic capital on a problem that did not affect Indonesia directly? Keen to coax Jokowi into taking action, one adviser made the case in terms that the president might accept more readily. Think about it from the perspective of a furniture exporter, he said. If the situation in the South China Sea escalates, then the cost of insurance for sea freight will rise, and it will be bad for their international business. 'When I put it like that, he got it,' the aide said, baffled but charmed at the same time.[12]

The adviser had stumbled upon an important lesson: if you want to understand Jokowi the politician, you must understand Jokowi the furniture maker. Biographers often try to paint psychological pictures of leaders based on their time in office. But their personalities, predilections, and peccadillos are largely established well before they get to power. That is even more so in the case of Jokowi.

There are few global leaders who have risen from obscurity as rapidly as Jokowi. In just nine years, he went from small-town businessman to president of the world's fourth most populous nation. It was an incredible turnaround for a simple boy from a simple family, in a country where politics has long been dominated by dynasties, tycoons, and the military.

When Jokowi first ran for the top job in 2014, many people argued that his surging popularity echoed that of Barack Obama, who lived in Jakarta for a few years as a schoolboy. But the comparisons end there, despite the physical likeness between the two men and the fact that they were born within two months of each other in 1961.

By his mid-30s Obama was a precocious graduate of Harvard Law School with lofty political ambitions and an acclaimed autobiography to his name. At the same age, Jokowi was running an unremarkable furniture factory in Solo, his hometown. While Obama was grappling with questions of race, identity, and politics, Jokowi was sourcing lumber supplies, overseeing sawmills, and touting his wares in broken English and an ill-fitting suit at international furniture expos. A better comparison would be to imagine, in the space of just nine years, someone going from second hand car dealer in Pittsburgh to president of the United States, or the owner of a shoe factory in Northampton becoming prime minister of the United Kingdom.

To understand how Jokowi did it, and why, we must go back to his roots in Solo. Jokowi often says that his approach to governing relies on 'going to the ground'. So, in the run-up to the 2014 presidential election, I took his advice and went to visit his factory, which has been managed by his brother-in-law since Jokowi became mayor of Solo in 2005. Set up in 1989, and named Rakabu after his first son, it was an unassuming operation, with dozens of employees producing solid but uninspiring wooden furniture for consumers around the world.

On my arrival, it was hot, humid, and noisy, with drilling and cutting machines drowning out the soft voices of the workers as I chatted with them. Everything was covered in a layer of sawdust and the factory buzzed with the rhythm of production. I watched as blocks of wood were hewn into slabs, the slabs made into planks, and the planks crafted into tables, chairs, and cabinets. And I started to understand not just how Jokowi had shaped this business, but how this business had shaped him.

In time, Indonesians and outsiders would come to see Jokowi as many different things: an economic liberal, a political reformer, a defender of pluralism and, eventually, a neo-authoritarian. But Jokowi has approached politics from a more straightforward perspective, that of the furniture maker. He needs electricity for his factory, roads and ports to move his goods, and ships to transport them to their overseas customers. He wants lower taxes and simpler regulations to make business easier, and better healthcare and education to ensure a happier and more productive workforce.

Over the years, I have asked Jokowi several times which political leaders he most admires. Each time, a quizzical look comes over his face before he brushes the question away. Despite Jokowi's perfunctory nods to Sukarno – the father of Indonesian independence and of Jokowi's quarrelsome party chair Megawati Sukarnoputri – he has never been the type to spend his evenings reading political biographies. In his own autobiography, ghostwritten by journalist Alberthiene Endah, he concedes that he had minimal interest in the world of politics before he became mayor of Solo.

Jokowi speaks most passionately not of vote-getting strategies or election wins but of his early days as an apprentice carpenter in the factory of his uncle, an early mentor. Miyono, who had built a successful business, told the young and wide-eyed Jokowi that he would never understand the wood business until he felt 'the vibrations of work from the most basic level'.[13] Jokowi took the advice to heart, returning home from work every day with his face and clothes caked in dust – and his appetite whetted to build a business of his own.

So, how did this pencil-slim, word-shy furniture maker catapult himself to the top of Indonesia's cut-throat political scene? To answer this question, we need to examine his early life in more depth. A major part of his electoral appeal, from Solo to the furthest jungles of Papua, is that he comes across as *merakyat*, or 'close to the people'. Like all successful politicians, he has massaged and honed this public image. But he has only been effective because the image is grounded in the gritty reality of his upbringing.

Jokowi was born in Solo, Central Java, in June 1961 in, according to his autobiography, the 'cheapest room' at the Brayat Minulya hospital. Many Indonesians could not afford a hospital birth at that time, so his family was certainly not destitute. But life was a struggle. His father, Notomiharjo, was a petty bamboo hawker, with paltry and irregular profits. The president-to-be was initially named Mulyono, but after suffering several illnesses, his parents changed his name in the hope of better fortune, as was the Javanese custom. Joko Widodo, as he was renamed, soon recovered – a 'mysterious' eventuality, as Jokowi puts it.

Jokowi was Notomiharjo's first and only son, but he was soon followed by three sisters. The family survived 'rupiah by rupiah', living in a succession of rented riverside shacks and suffering regular evictions.[14] It was an experience that would have two crucial consequences for Jokowi's later career as a politician. First, it allowed him to empathise with the tens of millions of Indonesians living in poverty, even in the wealthiest cities like Jakarta. Second, it made him understand the need for the state to offer basic services so that people could clamber out of the mire.

The president-to-be was inspired by the perseverance of his father, who took an extra job as a bus driver and roped in his wife and the young Jokowi to help run the furniture business. Notomiharjo was 'an example of how the little people struggle to survive without a helping hand from anyone', Jokowi said.[15] No-one had given his father funds to invest, a proper market stall for his trade, or help if he or his family were sick – all deficiencies that Jokowi would build his career on correcting.

Jokowi's political opponents have since attacked him for exaggerating the hardship of his early years, pointing to the hospital birth and the fact that his mother's brother was well-off. Without doubt, Jokowi has made the most of the harsher elements of his upbringing. His autobiography reads at times like a paean to the struggles and dignity of poverty. But there is no doubting that he is a self-made man who pulled himself up from modest beginnings. Unlike most of the business and political elites over whom he would later triumph, Jokowi was seen by Indonesians as someone like them. As he recounted in a campaign speech in Bogor in June 2014, a month before he was elected president: 'I never forgot where I came from; when I was young, I identified with the small people, I was one of them, and now it is time to do something for them.'[16]

It was not just Jokowi's family living in marginal conditions in the early 1960s. Indonesia itself was on the edge of collapse. Jokowi was born 16 years after Sukarno declared independence from the Netherlands, and only 12 years after the end of the bloody struggle to secure that independence. President Sukarno was running riot, having suspended Indonesia's first experiment with democracy in 1957, barely two years after the young nation's first general election. He was pushing *Konfrontasi* against Malaysia,[17] his newly independent neighbour, while simultaneously pulling Indonesia out of the United Nations, and stoking dangerous tensions between the powerful Indonesian Communist Party and the army.

Sukarno revelled in the disorder, believing that only he could unite the disparate peoples and forces that made up the world's biggest archipelagic nation. But the economy, about which he cared little and understood less, did not benefit from the chaos. Before Jokowi's sixth birthday, Sukarno was ousted after a low-profile general called Suharto took advantage of what was portrayed as an attempted coup by leftists in the military. Suharto then waged a terrifying campaign of mass murder that wiped out more than half a million alleged communists and their sympathisers, and set the stage for 32 years of autocratic rule.[18]

At the time, the young Jokowi thought little about politics; as far as we know, even these days he thinks little about political history. Indeed, he has made very few comments about the corruption and human rights abuses of the Suharto era. However, as Jokowi matured and moved into business, his view of the world was influenced by the shift to stability, order, and a focus on the economy under Suharto. Although Jokowi became president as the representative of the Sukarno family's political party, it would later become apparent that he had more in common with Suharto.

By the 1980s, with Suharto's technocratic reforms having better connected Indonesia's economy to the rest of the world, the fortunes of Jokowi's father were improving and he established a small furniture workshop of his own. Meanwhile, his son had grown his hair long, developed a lasting fondness for heavy metal bands like Metallica, and was studying forestry at Universitas Gadjah Mada, one of Indonesia's leading universities, in the nearby city of Yogyakarta.

Despite his taste in music, Jokowi was far from a rebel. While other students were risking everything to call out the flagrant abuses of the Suharto regime, Jokowi's understanding of politics was 'still at a low level'. Aside from occasional coffee-shop conversations about what was happening in Indonesia, he was more interested in climbing the awe-inspiring volcanoes of Java and the adjacent island of Sumatra.[19]

Upon graduation, the laconic young Jokowi took a job at a state-owned forestry company in Aceh, a restive but resource-rich province at the tip of Sumatra. After a few years in the field, he returned to Solo when his wife, Iriana, became pregnant. Having completed the apprenticeship in his uncle's factory, he decided to branch out on his own. He started his business in the late 1980s with hardly any capital, three workers, and a dogged determination to succeed.

The 15 years he spent building his business before he ran for the mayoralty of Solo were relatively uneventful and happy ones, compared with the political struggles he would face later. There were the usual financial highs and lows of any small business in its early years, of course. He was defrauded by unscrupulous customers and found it hard to get the loans he needed to expand beyond his small-time workshop. But, as he worked out how to harness the traditional artisanal skills of the carpenters in Central Java, he learned to improve his product designs to better suit burgeoning export markets.

While some underestimated Jokowi, the man with the village face and soft mannerisms, he had chutzpah. When he applied for a loan under a government program to help small businesses, he was offered just a quarter of the Rp500 million he had requested. He pushed back, telling them he wanted to 'make rice not porridge', and secured the loan he needed to go global.[20] He attended his first international furniture expo in Singapore in 1991 and soon became a regular on the circuit. He got his enduring nickname from a French client who wanted to distinguish him from all the other Indonesian salesmen called Joko.

A photograph from the period shows a diligent Jokowi manning his 'Rakabu Style' stall, while a foreign buyer examines his wares. Jokowi looks very much the small-town boy done good, sporting black trousers pulled high up his midriff, with an oversized brown suit jacket hanging off his spindly frame. He posted the picture on social media in 2019 to send a message: if he can do it, anyone can. Indonesia has the raw materials for success. It just needs hard work to get there.

*

By 2005, when he entered politics by running for mayor of Solo, Jokowi had done very well for himself. His business was thriving, he had become head of the local furniture makers' association, and his wife had opened a large wedding hall, which would soon double as a campaign event space. He had amassed personal wealth of nearly US$1 million.[21] In a country that had only just emerged from the wreckage of the Asian Financial Crisis of 1997–98, that put him well within the top 1 per cent wealth bracket. But, in terms of both affluence and character, he was still far from the gaudy tycoons and business-minded generals who would later bankroll his campaigns for the Jakarta governorship and the presidency.

Jokowi's success in business had given him self-confidence and taught him how to manage different types of people, from factory-floor workers and timber-plantation owners to foreign customers. Jokowi had built a good reputation locally, using his role at the industry association to give a leg-up to other small-business owners.

It was they who first suggested he run for office in 2005, as Indonesia prepared to hold its first-ever direct elections for local leaders. The elections were part of a series of democratising and decentralising reforms introduced in the wake of Suharto's fall in 1998.[22] 'If you can revitalise the spirits of weak businesses in our organisation, why don't you develop Solo?' a fellow furniture manufacturer asked Jokowi.[23]

In trying to unpick what drove him to enter politics, we come up hard against one of his many contradictions. In Jokowi's telling, his political apotheosis was effortless and unintentional. From Solo to Jakarta, to the presidential palace, he was simply a hard-working Everyman who was asked to do his duty and lead his people. It was 'destiny', he said. 'It's strange, the more I tried to avoid and reject that road, the more easily it unfolded in front of my eyes.'[24]

Given the messy style of his leadership today, it is easy to believe his claim that he entered politics 'without a plan'. However, it is much harder to believe in his faux humble insistence, which is typical of a Javanese leader, that he was devoid of political ambitions.

Even those who have worked with Jokowi for many years struggle to explain what has motivated him throughout his political career. I will examine in the next chapter how timing and luck (or fate, as Jokowi would see it) have played their part. His steady accomplishments in the furniture business put him on the local political radar just as Indonesia embarked on a bold new democratic experiment. His achievements in Solo propelled him into an ailing capital city that was desperate for a new type of leader who could get things done.

And finally, a vacuum at the top of politics, which was still dominated by tired dynastic scions and corruption-addled party hacks, sucked him into the presidency. By some combination of steely determination and sheer luck, he would make it to the top – accidentally on purpose.

CHAPTER TWO

Going to the ground to reach the top

The lackadaisical civil servants in Solo's city hall were in for a shock when Jokowi was elected mayor in June 2005. Not long after the 44-year-old arrived at the office on his first day, he stunned senior bureaucrats by ordering them to join him for a tour of the city's slums. His stated mission was to make the city hall workers extend free schooling to parents who could not afford the fees.[25]

But he also wanted to send a message to civil servants and voters that there was a new sheriff in town, and a new way of doing business. 'A work desk is only a place we come back to,' Jokowi told them. 'Our work is outside. We must see directly what is happening in the midst of the people.'[26]

This was Jokowi's first official *blusukan*, a Javanese word for the impromptu spot checks that would become his political stock-in-trade. The idea, as he told me on many occasions, was ridiculously simple: go to the people, ask what their problems are, and then solve them.

In the process, of course, he wanted to attract media attention, present himself as a man of the people, and light a fire underneath the sluggish bureaucrats who were holding back development. His pitch to renew Solo was encapsulated in his 2005 campaign slogan: '*Berseri Tanpa Korupsi*' or 'Brilliant Without Corruption'.[27]

Of course, Jokowi was not the first politician to try the man-of-action schtick. But there were two factors that set him apart. First, he had a real talent for retail politics – the more time he spent with voters, the more they warmed to him. Second, his assiduous focus on incremental improvements could deliver impressive results in a country where so many officials had been neglecting their duties for so long.[28]

By 'going to the ground', Jokowi would become a national phenomenon and rapidly find his way to the apex of Indonesian politics. Later, in Jakarta, he would be trailed on his spot checks by hundreds of local and international journalists. He would bring VIPs along for the ride, including then London Mayor Boris Johnson and Facebook Chief Executive Mark Zuckerberg.

When he became president, Jokowi's staff created a *blusukan* map on his website, tracking his visits across the country. However, once he was the commander-in-chief, surrounded by a phalanx of bodyguards, these supposed spot checks inevitably became more and more stage-managed. As Malcolm Turnbull noted after a sweat-drenched tour of a textiles market with Jokowi, 'there isn't a lot of room for impromptu performances in a presidential life'. [29]

Eventually, many Indonesians would start to wonder if there was less to his *blusukan* than met the eye. Was it an effective way to run a sprawling nation of more than 270 million people, or just a public relations exercise? But, in the early days, there was a folksy charm in his approach. It turned out to be so effective that it would change the course of Indonesian history, upsetting some of the country's most powerful politicians along the way.

This is not just the story of how a down-to-earth factory owner managed to become president of a great nation. It is also the story of Indonesia's second experiment with democracy – its flowering and, later, its withering on the vine. When Jokowi was elected mayor of Solo, it was just seven years since President Suharto had been ousted in the wake of the Asian Financial Crisis, after 32 years of autocratic rule.

Prior to that, Indonesia's founding president Sukarno had overseen a brief period of democratic rule in the 1950s. However, within two years of the 1955 legislative elections – independent Indonesia's first nationwide voting exercise – he became embittered by the country's divisive politics, and vowed to 'bury all the parties'.[30] Sukarno argued that Western-style liberal democracy, by which he meant a majority-ruled legislature with legal checks and balances, was not for Indonesia. Instead, he opted for 'Guided Democracy', an increasingly erratic and arbitrary form of personalised rule. After ousting Sukarno, Suharto would continue this domineering and nepotistic style, while holding stage-managed elections.

Jokowi's formative years as a young man and an emerging factory boss were all spent under some form of authoritarian rule. When he was elected in Solo, Indonesia had only ever known three sets of democratic national elections, in 1955, 1999, and 2004, when the first direct presidential election was held and Susilo Bambang Yudhoyono, known as SBY, triumphed. By 2019, at the time of Jokowi's re-election, Indonesia had organised three more sets of national and local elections, perfecting a fiendishly complex but mostly free and fair system that incorporated hundreds of thousands of candidates and millions of election workers.[31]

I will examine Jokowi's grasp of democracy and his commitment to the principles of good governance in a later chapter. In some disturbing ways, Jokowi has grown to share Sukarno's irritations with the strictures of democratic rule. What is important to understand at this point is how Jokowi seized on Indonesia's second democratic moment, embodying popular hopes for a better life and a government that listens more and does more for its people.

Blusukan is emblematic of one key element in Jokowi's political rise: his talent for retail politics. The other element is his ability to corral local, and then national, elites behind him. The tycoons, party bosses, religious leaders, and generals have brought him the money, political connections, and endorsements he has needed to capitalise on his connection to ordinary voters.

This balancing act has troubled political scientists eager to find overarching frameworks to explain trends in Indonesia. For a long time, as Jokowi's political bandwagon gathered pace, he was portrayed as a saviour of democracy and a hero of reform, the first president from outside the elite.[32]

Later, as he struggled in the presidential palace, he would be lambasted as a tool of oligarchic interests who had not only betrayed his own promises, but sold Indonesia down the river.[33] However, what has struck me is how little he has changed from his days as mayor of Solo.

The ascent of Jokowi swept many Indonesians and foreign friends into a frenzy of excitement about the potential for much-needed reform. But a closer and more dispassionate analysis of his rise to power reveals a man always playing both ends: the elite and the people. Does that make him a puppet or a fraud? Actually, it makes him a politician – and a good one.

Jokowi possesses another essential political skill: good timing. When he decided to run for mayor of Solo in 2005, he needed to find a political party to back him, a process known in Indonesian as *mencari perahu*, or 'seeking a vessel'. Various political parties were interested in Jokowi, including SBY's Democrat Party and two Islamic parties. But, fatefully, Jokowi opted for the Indonesian Democratic Party of Struggle (PDI-P), the party of former president Megawati. Representing itself as populist and pro-poor, it was a good fit for Jokowi's campaign style.

PDI-P was the strongest party in Solo, but it had a problem. Its putative candidate, moustachioed machine politician FX Hadi Rudyatmo, was a Christian in a city that was nearly three quarters Muslim. As such, it seemed difficult for him to win. PDI-P needed a Muslim to run for mayor, while FX Rudy could become the influential deputy.

Jokowi solved another issue for PDI-P, because his business connections brought funding for the campaign. His nose for a political opportunity and his ability to manage local elites won him the contested PDI-P nomination. And ultimately, it was his ability to connect with voters that won him the mayoralty, with 37 per cent of the vote, ahead of three other candidates.[34]

In his national campaigns in 2014 and 2019, Jokowi would win the votes of tens of millions of Indonesians by promising bureaucratic reform, job creation, improved infrastructure, and better access to health and education services. His 2005 election campaign in Solo, a city of 500000, was not that different. His rivals had also made vague promises to implement good governance reforms and reboot the economy. Like Jokowi, they sensed the desire for change in a city whose glory days as a sultanate seemed long past, overshadowed by the neighbouring city of Yogyakarta – to this day the only place in Indonesia where hereditary rule by the sultan endures.

What Jokowi did differently was campaigning. He showed off his ordinary origins with regular *blusukan*-style visits to markets and riverside *kampungs* (villages). He sought support from a wide range of the community groups that stitch together and enliven the fabric of Indonesian life. Jokowi reached out where others did not, meeting everyone from the parking attendants' association to local human rights NGOs, from Islamic groups to Catholic and ethnic Chinese ones.

The rolling jamboree of campaign events helped attract media attention at a time when Indonesian journalism was starting to flourish after the end of Suharto-era censorship. *Blusukan* not only sealed Jokowi's connection with ordinary voters, it gave journalists a good visual story and brought the national spotlight to his local endeavours.[35]

When Jokowi ran for governor of Jakarta in 2012 and the presidency in 2014, his campaign team lionised the achievements of his seven years as Solo mayor. To listen to them, it was as if he had single-handedly built a 'shining city on a hill'. They pointed to the way he had painstakingly convinced slum dwellers and street hawkers to abandon their informal perches for purpose-built homes and markets; the way he had increased investment by streamlining the byzantine business permit processes in city hall; and the way he had brought government closer to the people by making civil servants more responsive and ensuring that the poor could access hospitals and schools.

Jokowi had certainly made progress, but it was a long and hard slog. Rather than reforming the system at city hall or restructuring the bureaucracy, Jokowi pushed for incremental improvements, and he worked hard to monitor progress and solve problems as they arose. 'It took me three years to win civil servants' trust in Solo', Jokowi told me later. 'In Indonesia, leading by example is very important. If I show the example, others will follow.'[36]

This practical approach paid dividends. Solo was a troubled place before Jokowi took over. It was known as a city with a 'short fuse' because of its recent history of ethnic tensions, violent protests, and Islamic radicalism. These issues were fuelled by weak economic growth, poor employment prospects, and a lack of access to basic services, with fewer than half of the city's residents connected to the government water supply.[37] Jokowi didn't turn Solo into Singapore. It remained a raucous place. But it thrived, thanks to his leadership and the strong economic tailwinds that were lifting Indonesia out of the doldrums that followed the Asian Financial Crisis.

When I visited Solo in the run-up to the 2014 presidential election, it was hard to find anyone who would not sing Jokowi's praises.[38] Former residents of the Kampung Sewu slum told me how he had visited dozens of times to explain why they should leave their flood-prone shacks for new, purpose-built homes nearby. With a history of unscrupulous officials and developers evicting slum dwellers, as Jokowi himself had experienced, they were reluctant to move.

But they were won over by his persistence and his direct approach. 'Even when the road was full of mud, he still came to visit us,' one housewife told me as she and a friend showed me their new homes, small and basic but solid and accompanied by all-important land ownership certificates.

It was a similar story with the unlicensed traders who used to clog up the Banjarsari Park. Jokowi had engaged in tortuous talks to move them on as part of plans to beautify the city. Eventually, they relented and many saw their sales soar at the new, permanent market base. 'Jokowi is a good leader,' said one motorcycle parts dealer. 'He's brave enough to listen directly to the complaints of the market traders.'

Jokowi took a similar approach when he clashed with Solo's small but ardent pocket of hardline Islamists, telling me how he had refused to let them shout him down with a megaphone in a public meeting to discuss a building permit for a new church. When he approached them, they became much less vociferous in their objections, he said.[39]

Jokowi's advances in Solo were robust, but far from revolutionary. And yet his track record propelled him onto the national scene, due in part to the paucity of other good leaders during the first decade or so of Indonesia's second democratic experiment. At the national level, the same group of dynasties, businesspeople, and former generals still dominated politics. At a local level, the advent of elections for local assemblies and leaders had, in many places, simply democratised the opportunities for bribery, nepotism, and rank incompetence.[40]

Corruption remains widespread in Indonesia, which comes below China and India in Transparency International's ranking of global graft, and only slightly above Colombia.[41] Since its founding in 2002, Indonesia's Corruption Eradication Commission (KPK), which is admired by the public and feared by politicians, has prosecuted several hundred local leaders and parliamentarians, as well as government ministers, top judges, and tycoons.[42] Jokowi upset many activists and delighted many politicians in 2019 when he allowed the parliament to dilute the KPK's authority (see Chapter 5).

In the early years, however, Jokowi was seen as a rare icon of clean government. His steady progress in Solo soon attracted outside interest. In 2008, he was named one of Indonesia's best local leaders by *Tempo* magazine, the country's unrivalled leader in investigative journalism. In 2010 he won the Bung Hatta Anti-Corruption Award, named for Indonesia's founding vice president. And in 2011, Princeton University's Innovations for Successful Societies program started working on a case study about Jokowi's reforms in Solo.[43]

Cameron Hume, the US ambassador to Indonesia from 2007 until 2010, visited Solo in 2009 and left enthused by the 'dynamic and immensely popular mayor' who had 'proved that good governance is the secret to transforming a troubled society into a healthy one'.[44] He was impressed with the way Jokowi had taken the sting out of the city's radical Islamists, as well as spruced up the city and helped the economy to grow. Hume evidently sensed Jokowi's potential to go higher in politics, concluding that 'Solo is not unlike most of Indonesia, with tolerant hard-working people who just want government to give them an opportunity to make a living and to live their lives as they want'.

Jokowi, of course, was also playing Hume, as he started to believe that he could parlay his progress in Solo into national political success. The former exporter could see the long-term importance of foreign backing, particularly from the United States, and Hume left eager to help promote Solo and Jokowi in America and beyond. This knack for charming foreigners would prove indispensable to Jokowi later in his career.

If Jokowi was already flirting with thoughts of higher office, it was his landslide re-election in 2010 that convinced him he had what it took. By winning 90 per cent of the vote, he cemented his status as Indonesia's most promising local leader and a political outsider who could bend the system to his will.[45]

He got lucky two years later, when political party bosses searched for strong candidates to run for Jakarta governor, the nation's most influential local ruler. Megawati, the chair of Jokowi's party, and Prabowo Subianto, a former special forces general who had been married to one of Suharto's daughters, were looking to revive their political fortunes ahead of the 2014 presidential election.

Susilo Bambang Yudhoyono was mandated to step down as president after reaching the constitutional two-term limit, so this would be a 'clean slate' election. Megawati, with Prabowo as her vice-presidential candidate, had performed dismally in the 2009 election. Both Megawati and Prabowo, who ran his own party called Gerindra, thought that by nominating Jokowi for the Jakarta job they could use the rising star from Solo to launder their sullied political reputations ahead of 2014. As it happened, they proved too successful at talent-spotting and Jokowi would pip them at the post, showing that he could hold his own in the manipulative games played by the nation's top politicians.

The love-hate triangle between Megawati, Prabowo, and Jokowi, with the latter at the apex, would come to define the shape of Indonesian politics over the next decade, for better and for worse. Jokowi would fight two acrimonious elections against Prabowo before eventually absorbing his long-time rival into his cabinet in 2019. From the time of his nomination as a presidential candidate by PDI-P, Jokowi would tussle behind closed doors with Megawati and her advisers for influence over his cabinet choices and decision-making.

Jokowi's victory in Jakarta was not a sure thing. Well-connected incumbent Fauzi Bowo was the overwhelming favourite to win the election. The long-serving government official owned a Harley-Davidson motorbike, a Hummer SUV, and a Van Gogh painting. But he had little enthusiasm for improving the lives of the more than ten million inhabitants of Jakarta or tackling the city's gnawing problems, from floods and traffic jams, to mindless bureaucracy and corruption.[46] He did, however, have the backing of many of the nation's most influential power brokers, as he represented SBY's Democrat Party. This ultimately played into Jokowi's hands, boosting his claim to be the outsider who would shake up the old order and build a new Jakarta.

Recently arrived in Indonesia as a correspondent for the *Financial Times*, I followed Jokowi across the city on the campaign trail. Everywhere he went, people surged forward to get a look, to shake his hand or take a selfie: in the riverside shanties, where the city's vast and resilient underclass lives; at the makeshift markets where many of these people make their living; in the upmarket shopping malls, where the fast-expanding middle class enjoy concrete-laden Jakarta's version of public space; even at the five-star international hotels, where Indonesia's tight-knit community of tycoons, politicians, and foreign investors seek their own form of sanctuary.

Although it was these businesspeople and elite politicians who were funding Jokowi's campaign, he still pitched himself as the defender of the poor. 'Every month, I see the gap between the haves and the have-nots is increasing,' he told me in the back of his car after a frantic campaign stop at a textiles market in central Jakarta.[47] 'God has given me a chance to make this city better and I will start to change it from the slum areas, not from the centre.'

A few months later, after Jokowi won the election in a gruelling two-round process, his name immediately shot to the top of polls for possible presidential candidates in 2014, much to the chagrin of Megawati and Prabowo. Sitting down for a proper interview with a very happy Jokowi, I tried to tease out his political vision. But he batted away my suggestions that Jakarta and, by extension, Indonesia needed deep structural reforms to realise their potential. Instead, he offered a succinct summary of the furniture-maker's view of politics and economic development, which he still echoes today, six years into his presidency. 'We have natural resources and we have human resources,' he said. 'If we change the management of this city and the management of the country, then I think our country can grow better.'[48]

Jokowi's track record in Jakarta was limited because his term was so short. Fewer than 18 months after his inauguration as Jakarta governor in 2012, Megawati picked him as the PDI-P presidential candidate. For Jokowi's growing army of advisers and backers, his unofficial campaign for the presidency had begun on the day he was elected Jakarta governor. Jokowi skilfully manoeuvred into the orbit of Jakarta politics in order to accelerate his career before spinning off towards his ultimate destination.

The capital city faced many of the same problems as Solo, but on a much bigger scale – a corrupt and inefficient civil service, persistent floods, and some of Asia's worst traffic jams, thanks to the lack of a metro system. Jokowi, together with his tenacious Vice Governor Basuki Tjahaja Purnama, made early progress. Polluted rivers were cleaned up. The metro project was finally made shovel-ready after decades of delays. And local officials were pressured to improve their performance and stop demanding bribes for basic services such as issuing driving licences.[49] As in Solo, Jokowi also issued health and education cards, which helped the city's millions of poor residents connect to public services. But, as had been the case in Solo, the emphasis was on access rather than quality.

Following the new governor around Jakarta and, later, around the country on his presidential campaign, I was left with two conflicting sensations. On the one hand, Jokowi had an unrivalled ability to grab the attention and affections of Indonesian voters. His modest backstory and approachable manner made people believe he would deliver on his promises for cleaner government, better infra-structure, and improved public services. But, on the other hand, his approach to politics seemed disorganised and devoid of a strategy for how to achieve these reforms.

The very facets of his personality that made him such a good city mayor would, in the end, limit his ability to pull off the radical changes Indonesia needs. Jokowi thought that the more he eschewed the traditional ways of politics, the more popular he would become. He was right. After he was elected president in 2014, he explained his campaign tactics to a foreign academic. 'My program was: I am sim-ple, polite and honest. That's it. As long as people believed me, I was sure I would win.'[50]

As he rose through the ranks, Jokowi remained confident that he could carry on doing what he had always done. Some of his advisers, however, were starting to worry whether he truly understood the scale of the challenges that awaited him as presi-dent. His time in Solo and Jakarta had given him a taste of some of the thorniest issues, from reducing poverty to tackling Islamic radicalism. But he would find the challenges of national government to be far more complex. He would have to work with more than 30 ministries, as well as the unruly parliament and nearly 550 directly elected governors, mayors, and regents who, like Jokowi, all thought that they knew best.

On the campaign trail and in preparation for high-profile TV debates with his opponent Prabowo, Jokowi showed impatience when his team tried to coach him. He was not the sort of leader to read detailed briefs. Fearing for what was to come after he won the presidency, an adviser asked him how, as the leader of a country stretching more than 5000 kilometres east to west, he could continue to govern through *blusukan*. 'No problem,' the new president replied. 'Now I have a plane.'[51]

The remark encapsulated Jokowi's homespun charm and his need to demonstrate his composure to those close to him, as well as the public at large. When we met in his Jakarta office shortly after he won the 2014 presidential election, but before he was sworn in, I wondered if he were at all daunted by the prospect ahead of him. Quite the contrary, he told me, in between checking the city traffic on his CCTV feeds and taking congratulatory phone calls from world leaders. 'I'm calm, following the Javanese philosophy of *ojo kagetan* – don't get excited.'[52]

Jokowi had relied on his outsider status, his track record of incremental progress, and a healthy dose of luck to soar from a furniture factory in Solo to the presidential palace. But the shortcomings in that formula would be exposed in the merciless world of national politics. His unflappability would start to look like complacency. And the contradictions between his man-of-the-people image and his reliance on elite backers would become ever more apparent.

CHAPTER THREE

From outsider to father of a new political dynasty

When Jokowi decided to enter Indonesian politics in 2005, he wanted the blessings of his three teenaged children. He had sent them to study in Singapore, a luxury beyond the dreams of most Indonesians. When he called up Gibran Rakabuming Raka, his eldest son, he did not get the answer he wanted.

Gibran was unimpressed, as most teenagers would be. He told his father that if he were elected as mayor of Solo, he would not come to his events. 'Later, people will look at me as the son of an official,' he told Jokowi. 'I just want to be Gibran only.'[53] I met Gibran during the 2014 presidential campaign, at the behest of one of Jokowi's media advisers. The quiet young businessman seemed less than pleased with the attention as he reluctantly showed me around his catering company, Chilli Pari.

Jokowi was proud that Gibran, along with his brother Kaesang Pangarep and sister Kahiyang Ayu, had built their own small businesses without asking for their father's support, as is the norm for wealthy Indonesians. 'Becoming a president does not mean channelling power to my children,' he said in his 2019 autobiography, a veiled dig at the nepotism and corruption of the Suharto family.[54]

And yet, not long after Jokowi was re-elected as president in 2019, he moved to create his own dynasty. Not only did 32-year-old Gibran step forward to run for mayor of Solo, but Kahiyang's husband, Bobby Nasution, also said he would seek election as mayor of Medan, a booming city in North Sumatra. Both took up Jokowi's Indonesian Democratic Party of Struggle (PDI-P) flag.

Of course, Jokowi denied he was building a dynasty, insisting that 'everyone in Indonesia has the right to stand for election', just as they have a right to vote. He would not campaign for his children, he insisted, and it was up to the 'smart and discerning' Indonesian people if they were elected.[55]

In the broad context of Indonesia's post-independence history, it would be more surprising if Jokowi did not look to build a dynasty. Five out of Indonesia's six other presidents have offspring who followed them into politics, the only exception being BJ Habibie, a technocratic Suharto-era minister who was appointed as interim president when Suharto was ousted in 1998.

Looking beyond Jakarta, dozens of lower-profile dynasties proliferate at provincial, district, and city levels. The patriarchs of these dynasties, and the occasional matriarch, pass down their electoral offices, corrupt business deals, and nepotistic appointments from generation to generation as if they are the family silver – until, that is, the smart voters Jokowi mentioned occasionally get in the way.[56] Beyond Indonesia, political dynasties are the norm across Asia. There are too many to list, but take your pick of illustrious offspring ruling democracies and dictatorships alike, from Xi Jinping to Aung San Suu Kyi, and Shinzo Abe to Sheikh Hasina Wazed.

But Jokowi's political *raison d'être* was that he was different. To the wide-eyed human rights activists who helped carry Jokowi to the presidential palace, the entry of his son and son-in-law into politics was only the latest and most brazen example of how he had become an unscrupulous, transactional politician. The easy explanation for Jokowi's apparent transformation could be found in Lord Acton's adage that 'power tends to corrupt, and absolute power corrupts absolutely'.[57]

Robert Caro, the US journalist known for his painstakingly researched political biographies, put it better when he argued that 'power always reveals'.[58] The higher Jokowi rose from his obscure roots, the more his political contradictions were exposed.

In Solo, and to a lesser extent in Jakarta, he managed to keep his political machinations in the background and pitched himself implicitly as an anti-elite figure. He rarely made such grand claims explicitly. But it became impossible for him to sustain his outsider image once he decided to run for the presidency. Instead, he was revealed as a man with good political instincts and high electability, but no plan for how to manage the ranks of oleaginous politicos, tycoons, and generals that lined up around him as they sensed power shifting towards a new leader.

The first challenge, before Jokowi could run for president, was Megawati – a politician whose steeliness and stubbornness is matched only by her seeming simplicity. If she had not been the daughter of Indonesia's founding president, it is unlikely she would have become president herself. But even then, she had to rely on her predecessor, blind Islamic cleric Abdurrahman Wahid, being impeached and removed by the parliament. Indirectly elected in this manner in 2001, she lost Indonesia's first direct presidential election in 2004 to Susilo Bambang Yudhoyono. And she lost again to SBY in 2009, this time after selecting Prabowo Subianto as her running mate.

Not easily dissuaded, Megawati was contemplating another tilt at the top job in 2014, when SBY was constitutionally mandated to step down. While her party, PDI-P, routinely polled among the best of Indonesia's dozen or more political parties, her own ratings remained poor.[59] Her daughter Puan Maharani, by then a member of parliament, was also thinking about a run for the presidency, but suffered from the same lack of popularity.

Their weakness was Jokowi's opportunity. Once he was elected governor of Jakarta in September 2012, his popularity surged in nationwide surveys and there was a growing clamour for him to run for the presidency in 2014. That was partly down to his track record and his genuinely refreshing approach to politics. But it was also a result of the lack of other good candidates.

Prabowo, a brilliant tub-thumping rhetorician, was tainted by his links to the Suharto regime and extensive allegations of human rights abuses. Wiranto, another Suharto-era general with his own political party, also faced questions about his human rights record and was a much more wooden performer. Aburizal Bakrie, the other big name in the frame, was an unimpressive tycoon linked to a major environmental scandal.[60]

Indonesia's second experiment with democracy had, in many respects, been hijacked by the dark forces that had held the country back before. This was a consequence of the 'original sin' of *reformasi*, the reform movement that gave birth to the modern Indonesian state.

By opting for a process of graduated change from within rather than a revolution, Indonesia avoided the immense bloodshed and extreme uncertainty that would have accompanied efforts to truly dismantle the *ancien régime*. However, the price of a mostly smooth and peaceful transition has been to leave Suharto-era figures and institutions with a seat at the table. What is different today is that these players need to work through politicians who have genuine popular appeal in order to win in Indonesia's mostly free and fair elections.

To have a shot at the presidency, Jokowi had to engage in a delicate dance with Megawati and the loyal acolytes that surrounded her. If she wanted PDI-P to remain relevant, she needed his vote-getting powers. He needed her party, which was particularly strong in his home base of Central Java, to support his nomination. Jokowi successfully courted her with necessary displays of deference, 'opening doors for her, moving chairs, and even kissing her hand in public'.[61]

However, winning her affections would come at a price. Megawati's daughter Puan remained embittered that she had been passed over and would keep a tight hold on the PDI-P purse strings, almost terminally undermining Jokowi's presidential campaign in 2014.[62] And Jokowi would never escape the allegations that he was just a *boneka*, or 'puppet', whose strings were being pulled by Megawati.

The cost of upsetting Puan became obvious to me as I followed Jokowi around Indonesia on the campaign trail in 2014. With PDI-P not backing Jokowi wholeheartedly, in terms of funds or boots-on-the-ground, he had to rely on loose networks of grassroots volunteers. That gave his campaign an earthy feel but deprived it of coherence. In reality, it was chaos, a taste of what was to come when this man of action got his feet under the presidential desk.

On one occasion, I arrived at night in Surabaya, an industrial city in the key electoral battleground of East Java, with no idea of where exactly Jokowi was going to be the next day. I couldn't have known because his team hadn't decided yet. Early the next morning, I jumped in a rented car, went to Jokowi's hotel, and told the driver to follow the *rombongan*, or 'entourage', as it raced through the region's crowded streets at a terrifying pace. If we had slowed down, we would have lost the group and had no clue where they were going.

Sitting in the lead car behind the police outriders, Jokowi tossed campaign t-shirts (which read '*Jokowi adalah kita*', or 'Jokowi is one of us') out of the window as people stepped out of their homes and shops to see what was going on. Every now and then, he would stop at a mosque or a market and spark a crush that was almost as threatening to my safety as the driving.

That evening, he was due back in Surabaya for a concert by Slank, a popular rock band that have been among his strongest supporters. He was hours late, not that the attendees, some of whom had travelled hundreds of kilometres to be there, seemed to mind. They told me what so many of his backers did, that this clean, humble, and honest man deserved their support, no matter what.

Fewer than two weeks out from the election, Jokowi had squandered a poll lead of as much as 30 percentage points over Prabowo, who was approaching level-pegging.[63] The former army special forces commander and his team fought an effective, if dirty, ground game, capitalising on his experience of counter-insurgency and black operations from Papua to East Timor.[64]

I watched Prabowo at several large rallies, where he flew in on his own helicopter before giving explosive nationalistic speeches, accusing his opponent of being backed by unnamed 'foreign lackeys'.[65] The Prabowo campaign also attacked Jokowi by spreading disinformation that falsely claimed he was ethnically Chinese, a Christian, and a communist – three Cs bound to lose him support.[66] With social media campaigning yet to take off in many areas, the best vehicle for this slander was not Twitter or Facebook (as would become the case later), but a fake tabloid newspaper distributed in key voter battlegrounds in Java.

When I sat down for an early morning chat with Jokowi the day after I had chased his convoy around East Java, he seemed relaxed and brushed off concerns about the poll numbers and Prabowo's slurs. 'I know the maths,' he said. 'I'm very confident we can win.'[67] As for the chaotic campaign, that was the way he operated, with enthusiastic volunteers or, as he put it, 'organisation without form'.

You would, of course, expect a candidate days out from a presidential election to claim that they would win. But Jokowi seemed genuinely convinced that his connection with voters and his prior momentum would carry the day. It was that faith, several of his advisers told me, that was part of the problem. The flipside of his cocksure confidence was that he was not keen to listen to advice. It was a tendency that would prove much more damaging once he was sitting in the presidential hot seat, facing an in-tray of intractable problems.

Before you can make sense of Jokowi's presidency, you must understand a little about the morass of political parties he had to negotiate to secure power and govern. There are currently nine parties in Indonesia's 575-seat main parliamentary body, the Dewan Perwakilan Rakyat (DPR), or People's Representative Council. Some 16 parties contested the 2019 legislative elections, which were held on the same day as the presidential election. If that seems like a lot, it still represents a significant streamlining from the first election after the fall of Suharto in 1999, when 48 parties contested and 21 won seats.[68]

Unhelpfully for outsiders looking for straightforward analytical frameworks, there are no easy dividing lines over ideology or policy. There is no left-wing versus right-wing split, as we see in many democracies. The parties have similar views on the economy, broadly wanting a bigger role for the state compared to the private sector, and tending towards protectionism. When it comes to governing, parties tend to form large 'rainbow' coalitions designed to divvy up the spoils of office, rather than create shared policy platforms. This process has been called 'party cartelization, Indonesian-style'.[69]

The most apparent fissure is between the Islamic parties and the rest, which are sometimes called nationalist or secular, both terms that fail to capture the complexity of their views.[70] Four of the nine parties in the current DPR, holding 30 per cent of the seats, are considered Islamic, and their members say they want to see a bigger role for Islam in politics. Of the rest, PDI-P has the strongest commitment to maintaining pluralism and diversity.

However, the divide often breaks down in practice. So-called nationalist parties have been at the forefront of promoting Shariah regulations at a local level and Islam-friendly policies at a national level. At the same time, Islamic parties often put issues other than religion front and centre.[71] For example, the Prosperous Justice Party is one of the most ardent Islamic parties, but its main campaign promises in 2019 were populist pledges to abolish the motorcycle tax and make it easier to get a driving licence.[72]

Some of the parties are vessels for the ambitions of individual politicians, including Prabowo's Gerindra and SBY's Democrat Party. PDI-P is partly a family fiefdom, but has a broad base of support in Java built on Sukarno's legacy of populist nationalism and its role as an opposition party during the Suharto years. Other parties have grown out of or lean towards specific mass organisations, including the National Awakening Party, which is linked to the Nahdlatul Ulama, a Muslim organisation with tens of millions of members, and the National Mandate Party, which is connected to Muhammadiyah, a rival Islamic group. The party with perhaps the strongest organisational roots is Golkar, which was Suharto's political vehicle and has transformed itself into a successful player in the competitive elections of the post-*reformasi* era.

Although they differ in size, spread, and quality, the parties all lack effective institutional mechanisms for debating policy, raising funds, and training their members. They do not fill the traditional role of political parties in a democratic system: connecting voters with the government, simplifying election choices, and organising and executing policymaking.[73] They operate more as vote-getting machines at election time and patronage distribution machines once in power. It is little wonder that

Indonesians consider their political parties to be among the nation's most corrupt institutions. Many voters today would share Sukarno's desire, stated in 1956, to 'bury all the parties'.

In the aftermath of Jokowi's remarkable 2014 election victory, in which he achieved 53 per cent of the vote to Prabowo's 47 per cent, some of his team urged him to transform his tens of thousands of devoted volunteers into his own party.[74] It would have been very hard, given new laws designed to reduce the number of parties. Yet, some saw it as the only way to free him from the grip of Megawati and the other elite politicians and bureaucrats who were likely to stymie reform efforts.[75]

His advisers should have known that Jokowi was not one to take such radical steps. Instead, he took a similar approach to his predecessor, SBY, slowly building a big tent coalition designed to parcel out patronage and minimise opposition, rather than make government more effective. Jokowi, who had vowed during the 2014 campaign to reject horse-trading (known as *dagang sapi*, or 'cow-trading' in Indonesia), was to prove a master of building large party cartels.

When he was sworn in as president in 2014, he was backed by four parties that held 40 per cent of the DPR seats. But within two years, he had brought four more parties into his coalition, including the power brokers of Golkar and the Hanura party of Wiranto, giving him nearly 70 per cent of DPR seats.[76] Following the 2019 election, when Jokowi sensationally brought Prabowo back into the fold after two bitterly fought presidential contests, Jokowi's coalition held three quarters of the DPR seats.

This was an impressive feat of transactional politics. On the good days, when Jokowi seemed to be in control of his fractious coalition, the factory owner from Solo took pleasure in his ability to get one over the conniving politicians of Jakarta. Over a bowl of noodles at the presidential palace a few months after his inauguration in 2014, a chuckling Jokowi told me how Fadli Zon, the deputy DPR speaker and one of Prabowo's toughest political outriders, had approached him to make peace. 'He came to see me holding a copy of *Time* magazine with me on the front and asked me to sign it,' Jokowi said.[77]

But the perpetual coalition building did little to improve his government's performance. As one veteran observer of Indonesian politics explained, 'when everything is a transaction among factions of the same elite, policy ambiguity is almost inevitable'.[78] In the DPR, Jokowi's large majority has still not translated into an effective coalition. Unlike in parliamentary systems such as the United Kingdom or Australia, Indonesian ministers are often not members of parliament, so even those in Jokowi's cabinet who represent political parties struggle to wield authority over their respective DPR factions.

Each of the supposedly governing parties spends as much time fighting with each other as they do cooperating. US president Lyndon Baines Johnson famously retained the services of J Edgar Hoover, the manipulative FBI director, because it was 'better to have him inside the tent pissing out, than outside pissing in'.[79]

In Indonesian politics, you can bring the political parties into your tent, but you cannot hope to control the direction in which they piss. Many decisions, in any case, are made in backroom deals on issue-based parliamentary committees, rather than majority votes of the whole DPR. This reflects a political culture that prioritises *musyawarah* and *mufakat* – 'deliberation' and 'consensus' – over sound policymaking.[80]

The interminable problems in the DPR were compounded by Jokowi's ministerial selections. From the dreamy idealism of 2014 to the more prosaic 2019 election victory, his cabinets have been a mix of the good, the bad, and the ugly. His choices have been shaped by compromises with

Megawati and the wider party cartel as much as his own preferences. The president has shown a liking for maverick outsiders. But he tends to let them go when they attract too much attention. That was the fate that befell outspoken ministers such as Susi Pudjiastuti (fisheries), Ignasius Jonan (energy), and Anies Baswedan (education), the last of whom became a powerful opponent of Jokowi after his abrupt dismissal in 2016.

The impressive technocrats led by Finance Minister Sri Mulyani Indrawati, previously number two at the World Bank, have been counterbalanced by a litany of ineffective or questionable characters. There was Rachmat Gobel, the protectionist trade minister who claimed that imports of second-hand clothes could spread HIV,[81] and Terawan Agus Putranto, the health minister who said God would protect Indonesia from COVID-19.[82] Then there were the former generals, Prabowo and Wiranto, accused of past human rights abuses.[83] Beyond these two, Jokowi increasingly turned to ex-military figures, including long-time business partner Luhut Pandjaitan, as his struggles mounted.

In the eyes of Jokowi's supporters from civil society – the original true believers – it was a steady fall from grace once he entered national politics. Compromises with Megawati begat compromises with other political parties and tycoons. That diluted the potential purity of Jokowi's ministerial teams, which made him unable to deliver reform or uphold his pledges to fight corruption and investigate past human rights abuses. A leading pollster concluded that, after his first year in the palace, Jokowi was 'a weak president caught between reform and oligarchic politics'.[84]

From the activists' perspective, it was downhill from there. As I will explore later, the mobilisation of hardline Islamist opposition in Jakarta prompted Jokowi to take an increasingly authoritarian turn and, as a result, he became ever more entrenched with the elites and distant from his grassroots origins. The activists see Jokowi's transactional politics, and the creation of his own dynasty, as a sign of character weakness. However, it seems to me that, as Robert Caro put it, power had revealed the man's true nature rather than corrupted it.

As I argued earlier, a close look at his track record in Solo shows that Jokowi has always been a pragmatist rather than an idealist. He is a leader driven by action, not ideas. And yet it was the promise of structural change that carried him from the backstreets of Solo to the world stage. How then to square these two Jokowis: the political outsider, and the father of a new dynasty? The answer lies in a heavy dose of realism about the nature of both Indonesia and the man.

'Indonesian politics is about seducing people with profits, not ideas and ideology,' one of Jokowi's ministers told me.[85] 'Jokowi wants to be as much as possible to as many people as possible.' However, he added, once Jokowi became president and was facing a far more complex array of challenges, he struggled to recreate the intensity of his city-government years and became much more reactive. His 'chameleon-like' approach to politics started to look less like a strength and more like a weakness.

The one area where the former factory owner did focus his energies was on the economy and infrastructure development. And here we would see another series of contradictions emerge: between his calls to expand foreign investment and his pro-tectionist instincts; between his professed mastery of micromanagement and his capricious nature; and between his desire to streamline bureaucracy and his unwillingness to upset the established order.

CHAPTER FOUR

Building the economy: A hard-hat president chases dreams

The president's aide looked at his watch with a grimace as my meeting, which had started several hours late, continued to run over time. He suggested that Jokowi wrap up, but the president waved him away. 'No, it's better I show you,' he told me as he went through slide after slide of infrastructure projects on his computer.

The Trans-Sumatra Toll Road? It had been extended by another 13 kilometres since his last visit, with the construction team moving to three shifts a day. The Pemalang–Batang Toll Road in Central Java? After eight years of setbacks because of problems with land acquisition, Jokowi had finally kicked it into action a few months earlier. That was nothing compared to the Jatigede Dam in West Java, delayed for similar reasons for

40 years, until the president had intervened, of course.

By this point, his aide had gone from irritation to resignation as the daily schedule went off course yet again – a regular occurrence in the Jokowi palace. But the king of infrastructure was not done. He had saved the best for last: the Jakarta Mass Rapid Transit, or MRT.

Jokowi commenced the construction of Indonesia's first-ever metro line when he was governor of the capital, and phase one was eventually completed in 2019 thanks to his successor, and former running mate, Basuki Tjahaja Purnama. 'I always check this project,' he added with a smile of self-satisfaction. For Jokowi, it was a symbolic marker to show that decades of mismanagement were being left behind and Jakarta was finally joining the ranks of proper world cities with public transportation.[86]

The president loves infrastructure. It is hard to imagine any other leader of a major country taking such delight in the minutiae of construction projects. It is the one aspect of his various programs and manifestos that he has always embraced personally, and delivered on, from Solo to Jakarta to the presidential palace. One of the defining images of his presidency is Jokowi in a hard hat and high-visibility vest breaking ground with a shovel or inspecting workers as they put the finishing touches on the latest airport, port, or railway.

The obsession is partly a consequence of his bias to action, thinking like a mayor more than a president. It is also partly a consequence of his nuts-and-bolts understanding of the economy, developed during his years in the furniture business. Above all, it is a response to Indonesia's overwhelming need for better infrastructure to move its economy into the fast lane.

Jokowi's predecessor, Susilo Bambang Yudhoyono, benefited from several years of commodity price-fuelled growth, as China's demand for Indonesian coal, rubber, and palm oil surged in the mid-2000s. But, complacent and indecisive, he failed to use the good years to expand the country's traffic-clogged roads or upgrade its inefficient harbours and air-ports. That left economic growth stuck at around 5 per cent per year. That looks solid. But Indonesia was not generating enough investment to create jobs for its fast-growing population, with more than two million young people entering the workforce every year.[87]

Besides the inadequate physical infrastructure, the other main hurdle to increasing the level of foreign and domestic investment was poor regulation. When he was Jakarta governor, Jokowi complained bitterly about the 'ridiculous' number of ministerial approvals he needed to begin work on the first line of the MRT. 'That's why many officials just say: we can't do these big projects, it's too complicated,' he told me after I followed him on a tour of a new night market. 'If it's hard for the government, imagine the problems for the private sector.'[88]

Much of my time as a foreign correspondent and think-tank analyst covering Indonesia has been spent listening to grizzled executives complain about nonsensical laws, rapacious bureaucrats, and profit-killing ministerial diktats. Examples range from the absurd, such as a thriving tech start-up that was obliged to buy a typewriter to fill in its tax forms, to the sublimely unjust, with foreign company employees jailed on dubious charges after upsetting the wrong people.[89]

Jokowi, who has been courting foreign investors since his Solo days, is serious about tackling the twin problems of bad infrastructure and bad regulation. It is not just about helping his elite backers in the business world. He believes that higher growth is essential to create more jobs and a more just society. Millions of Indonesians, including Jokowi, have become wealthy in the recession-free years after the Asian Financial Crisis. But tens of millions have been left behind in one of Asia's most unequal societies.[90]

Indonesia still suffers from high levels of deprivation, although the official poverty rate declined from 11 per cent when Jokowi became president, to just over 9 per cent when he was re-elected in 2019.[91] Many Indonesians live in a kind of economic purgatory, hovering above the poverty line, but liable to fall back below it when hit by a family illness, cyclical downturn, or some other misfortune. When COVID-19 broke out in Indonesia in early 2020, the finance minister warned that it would set back the struggle against poverty by a decade.[92]

Only 52 million Indonesians are classed as 'economically secure' by the World Bank.[93] The other 80 per cent of the population lives closer to the edge, scraping by as subsistence farmers, informal construction workers, and food-cart operators. Unless the government can generate enough decent jobs for these people, Indonesia's much vaunted demographic dividend, the result of its young, growing population, risks becoming a demographic time bomb.

Jokowi knows that he needs better infrastructure and regulation to get higher growth rates, create more high quality jobs, and generate more revenue to pay for the health and education services he has promised. Having put the economy at the centre of his presidency, his legacy will to a great extent be defined by how he delivers on these pledges.

Few economists doubt that Indonesia has the potential to grow much faster, even if it will struggle to reach the heights that Jokowi spoke of in his re-inauguration speech in 2019. However, politics is a practical art, not a theoretical science. Jokowi began his time in office with concrete progress on infrastructure development, but the hard-hat president risks being derailed by his pursuit of unrealistic dreams.

His decision to build a new capital city is testament to his whimsical nature and his disorganised governing style. He has made some progress streamlining business regulations, but his endless talk of reform hides a much deeper contradiction between his desire for foreign investment and his protectionist instincts. After his re-election in 2019, Jokowi said he could pursue difficult economic reforms because Indonesia's two-term limit left him free of the 'burden' of seeking re-election.[94] But it is far from clear what kind of reforms, and what kind of economy, Jokowi really envisions.

Disheartened by the lack of progress under SBY, many investors, journalists, and foreign governments have seen the Jokowi they want to see: a liberal economic reformer who will finally set the good ship Indonesia on the correct course. It is a tendency that I, as a reporter, tried and sometimes failed to resist. And it is a perception Jokowi and his advisers are happy to maintain, at least when it comes to outsiders with cash to splash. While going through his infrastructure slideshow at the palace, he was keen to tell me, and by extension the influential investors who read the *Financial Times*, that he was committed to building an economy that was 'open and competitive'.[95]

However, Jokowi's focus on infrastructure is not driven by an ideological commitment to free-market economics. He is just as indifferent to economic theory as he is to political theory. Rather, he is a developmentalist like Suharto, who believed that economic growth was necessary to maintain political legitimacy.[96] But without a lucid vision of how he wants to remake the economy, Jokowi has struggled to overcome a fundamental contradiction that has held back Indonesia since independence: the country needs foreign investment and know-how to develop, but economic liberalism is seen as a tool of colonial oppression.

Jokowi's obsession with shepherding the progress of building projects falls far short of being a strategy to remake the economy. He has struggled to scale up individual successes into the coherent program that Indonesia needs if it is to realise its potential and ensure a decent future for the tens of millions still living on the edge.

Wary of giving those around him too much power, Jokowi eschews the sort of central policy delivery unit that many governments rely on to monitor and implement changes. There are various organisations and ministries that are meant to have such a coordination role.

The Committee for the Acceleration of Priority Infrastructure Delivery was set up in 2014 to oversee economic development projects alongside the National Planning Ministry, the Finance Ministry, the Public Works Ministry, and the Coordinating Ministry for Economic Affairs. The State Secretariat, which has its own minister, and the presidential office, are meant to provide another layer of central command and control.

However, the abundance of such entities is a sign of their relative weakness. Ministers compete as much as they cooperate. And Jokowi runs the palace more as an imperial court than a chief executive's office, leaving ministers and advisers guessing as to his intentions and, not infrequently, taking big decisions on a whim.

One former minister in SBY's government, who was initially supportive of Jokowi, said that the president increasingly acted 'like a king'. 'Jokowi's ministers are scared to challenge his decisions,' he told me.[97] 'That's different from SBY. He was indecisive, so when he was criticised, he would re-think. Not so with Jokowi.'

The president prefers to rely on personalities rather than processes. He has leaned on a small and sometimes rotating cast of fixers to get things done. Chief among them is former general and businessman Luhut Pandjaitan, who Jokowi first met in 2007 when they set up a wood processing venture together.[98] Having recognised Jokowi's political potential at an early stage and supported his campaigns, Luhut has been rewarded with an increasing set of responsibilities: he started as chief of staff after the 2014 election, but ended up as coordinating minister for maritime affairs, with wide-ranging formal and informal powers.

After his re-election in 2019, Jokowi expanded Luhut's narrow-sounding but powerful portfolio even further to include oversight of investment, cabinet decisions, and priority national projects.[99] Luhut's star has continued to rise, earning him many fans as well as detractors.[100] By contrast, others who have momentarily had the president's ear on economic issues – including first-term Vice President Jusuf Kalla and Finance Minister Sri Mulyani – have seen their power in the palace wax and wane.

While those around him jostled for influence, Jokowi raced around the country opening airports, ports, and bridges. Images of the president with a shovel in hand or riding a motorcycle down a new road were beamed around the country daily. However, his greatest strength would become a weakness as Jokowi prioritised action over quality and planning.

By the start of his second term, he seemed to be suffering from what Indonesia's neighbours in the Philippines called an 'edifice complex', named after former first lady Imelda Marcos' infatuation with funding grand new buildings regardless of their efficacy.

When Jokowi decided, against the advice of several cabinet members, to pursue impulsive and expensive plans to build a new capital city in the jungles of Kalimantan, advisers shook their heads in despair. But they were not surprised.

'Jokowi doesn't like analysis, he likes action and decisions,' one adviser told me. 'There was no proper analysis of which infrastructure projects would boost growth and productivity the most. Instead he just pushed projects depending on where he was visiting.' This haphazard approach is the flipside of Jokowi's *blusukan* style. In his telling, he is not satisfied by 'reading data alone' but needs to 'see, feel and believe'.[101]

Jokowi's hasty decision-making, desire for media-friendly project launches, and inability to find a stable balance between economic nationalism and openness often created problems. In April 2017, the president travelled to the Philippines for a summit of the Association of Southeast Asian Nations (ASEAN) and bilateral talks with his maverick Philippines counterpart, Rodrigo Duterte. Both former city mayors who had committed to building more infrastructure, the men wanted to cap their visit by unveiling a signature project.

They opted for a new ferry route between General Santos, at the southern tip of the Philippines' Mindanao Island, and the Indonesian port of Bitung in North Sulawesi, around 500 kilometres away. It had been discussed for years, with numerous studies funded by foreign aid agencies and ASEAN highlighting it as a linchpin project. The idea was to boost trade by cutting shipping times between the two bustling port cities from days to hours, with traffic no longer routed back via distant Jakarta and Manila.[102] As the two leaders banged a ceremonial gong at the departure of the first ferry, Duterte called it a 'historical milestone'.[103] For Jokowi, it was meant to be concrete evidence that his plan to make Indonesia into a 'global maritime fulcrum' (see Chapter 6) was gathering pace.

Yet, when I travelled to North Sulawesi a few months later to follow up on the project, I learned that the ferry had never made another journey. Local officials and businesspeople told me that the Indonesian trade ministry was reluctant to open North Sulawesi to competition from the Philippines, and had restricted the products that could be imported via the route. And the government had failed to work out a plan with the local community for how to make the ferry sustainable. So, with hardly any customers and no government support, the shipowner had cancelled the route. Well-intentioned but poorly executed, it was a metaphor for the way Jokowi's government managed the economy.

Although his government lacked coherence, there were good decisions as well as bad. Much of the infrastructure Jokowi championed was sorely needed and delivered on schedule, including the first line of the Jakarta metro. Overall, he increased the infrastructure budget from Rp270 trillion in 2016 to Rp400 trillion by 2019.[104]

Early on in his first term, Jokowi made the tough call to cut costly fuel subsidies, which were burdening the budget and providing most benefit to well-off car owners. When Jokowi's predecessor SBY had come under pressure to do the same, he prevaricated, in typical fashion, fearful of street protests.

Jokowi also brought back Sri Mulyani, Indonesia's best-known economist, from her executive role at the World Bank and made her finance minister again. She has worked hard to try to lift Indonesia's tax revenues, which are smaller than those of Cambodia, Liberia, and Bolivia when measured as a proportion of gross domestic product.[105] Her steady hand on the tiller has kept Indonesia's finances under control, avoiding the sort of debt accumulation that preceded the Asian Financial Crisis. But she does not have the power to drive transformative change.

Jokowi appointed other technocrats, including private equity investor Tom Lembong, first as trade minister and then as investment minister, to improve economic efficiency and attract foreign investment. With his and Mulyani's input, Jokowi would launch more than a dozen so-called economic stimulus packages in his first term.

These misleadingly titled measures were designed to streamline business-permit processes, a Jokowi bugbear since his factory days, and expand foreign investment in certain select sectors. By reforming these rules, Indonesia leapt up the World Bank's closely watched 'ease of doing business' ranking from 120th to 73rd place during Jokowi's first five years as president.[106] Yet, I couldn't find many businesspeople who believed that investing in Indonesia had actually become any easier during that period.

The problem was twofold. First, there was a lack of coordination across government, which wasn't unique to Jokowi, but was exacerbated by his ad hoc leadership style. A year into his presidency, one of Jokowi's ministers warned that inter-ministerial jealousy – known in Indonesia as *ego sektoral* – was the government's 'common enemy'.[107] Jokowi would bump up against it time and again.

For example, in 2018 he called for foreign workers' visa requirements to be simplified, only for bureaucrats to come back with new regulations that would in fact make it harder for companies to employ the foreign experts they needed.[108] The economists and technocrats who worked in then Vice President Jusuf Kalla's office, which doubled as an unofficial policy unit, had to unpick the new regulations to work back to Jokowi's original intention.[109]

Another telling case of *ego sektoral* cropped up after Jokowi's re-election in 2019, when he had pledged to support the growth of Indonesia's burgeoning tech sector. As a signal of intent, he appointed Nadiem Makarim, the 35-year-old

Harvard graduate who founded Gojek, Indonesia's top ride-hailing and food delivery app, as his education minister. But just a couple of months into his second term, the trade ministry came out with a typically vague and non-business friendly regulation on e-commerce that executives said would stymie the industry's prospects.[110]

The second major problem was a failure to strike a durable balance between economic openness and protectionism. Darmin Nasution, then the coordinating minister for economic affairs, stumbled across the conundrum at the launch of the 16th economic stimulus package. Like the other packages, it was designed to promote foreign investment. But Darmin felt the need to deny that this package was 'pro-foreigner', suggesting instead that it was designed to reduce Indonesia's reliance on imports. 'This republic is over 70 years old yet there are so many things that we do not have,' he said. 'As our economy has grown, our imports have exploded because we are not able to provide the goods ourselves.'[111]

The president, too, would swerve wildly between charm offensives with foreign investors and domestic promises to wean Indonesia off imports and foreign companies. Although he often spoke of the need to expand trade, his government erected non-tariff barriers, such as the restrictions on e-commerce, with as much regularity as its predecessors.[112]

Jokowi was skilled at helping people see what they wanted. Foreign investors working with him in Solo and Jakarta saw a city official who wanted to make their lives easier. Indonesians were more taken with Jokowi's economic nationalism, such as his early support for the production of a national car, a disastrous project from which he backed away after using it to grab media attention in Solo and Jakarta.[113]

Once Jokowi was running the nation, it became much harder to maintain these contradictory positions without paying a price. Passing 16 reform packages and moving up the World Bank rankings will not attract many foreign investors if you are simultaneously prioritising the development of inefficient state-owned enterprises (SOEs) and nationalising some of the country's biggest energy projects. But that is exactly what Jokowi did.

Today, Indonesia has more than 100 SOEs, which employ hundreds of thousands of people and dominate large swathes of the economy, from transport, banking, and electricity to fertiliser production and pawn shops.[114] These SOEs are more pervasive in

Indonesia than in any other major economy apart from China.[115]

From the outset, Jokowi saw them as a useful tool to accelerate his plans to develop infrastructure and boost economic growth without affecting the national budget. He hoped, too, that as state entities they could negotiate the usual regulatory minefields with more alacrity than foreign investors. 'If we invest Rp10 trillion in roads through the public works ministry, we only get Rp10 trillion,' he told me in 2015. 'But if we give the SOEs Rp10 trillion in capital, they can use it to borrow money from the bank and invest Rp70 trillion.'

The problem was that many of these companies were badly managed and riddled with corruption. Advancing their interests meant squeezing out the more efficient private sector, both domestic and foreign. Jokowi leaned on the SOEs without a tight enough grip on their behaviour. The inevitable result was that by 2019, the president had to bring in a successful businessman, former Inter Milan owner Erick Thohir, to clean up the financial and legal mess they had made.[116]

In the natural resources sector, Jokowi pushed ahead with the nationalisation of key foreign-developed projects, from the huge Grasberg gold and copper mine in Papua, formerly controlled by

US group Freeport McMoRan, to the large Mahakam gas block, formerly owned by France's Total. Jokowi took over these blocks legally – rather than confiscating them as Sukarno might have done – but only after Indonesian officials had worn down the foreign investors with interminable disputes over contracts and permits. If Jokowi wants to intensify this process and deepen the role of the nation's influential SOEs, he is well within his rights. The problem is his inability to establish a steady balance between the state and private sector.

It is striking how the legacy of post-colonial hostility to economic liberalism still holds such sway today, despite Indonesia's need for foreign capital and technology. In a fiery speech on Independence Day in 1963, Sukarno set out his 'very simple' view of economic development, versions of which have regularly passed the lips of Jokowi and many of his ministers. To succeed, Sukarno argued, all Indonesia needs to do is stand on its own two feet. That is because it has such an abundance of natural resources, a large and hardworking population, and a history of illustrious pre-modern trading empires whose tentacles reached across the seas from China to Africa.

'If nations who live in a dry and barren desert can solve the problems of their economy, why can't we?' he asked. Of most importance, from Sukarno's perspective, was self-respect and self-reliance, as no great nation should 'beg' for assistance from foreigners. It is, he said, 'better to eat poverty rations of cassava and be independent than eat beefsteak and be enslaved'.[117]

Decades of subsequent failed efforts to become self-sufficient in beef production would show that Indonesians, in fact, preferred to eat foreign beef while simply complaining about it. But the hostility to economic liberalism went beyond Sukarnoist rhetoric.

Article 33 of the Indonesian Constitution, which foreign investors would do well to read, establishes that 'the economy shall be organised as a common endeavour based upon the principles of the family system'. It also stipulates that 'sectors of production which are important for the country' and 'land, waters and natural resources' will be 'controlled by the State', with the latter also used 'to the greatest benefit of the people'.[118] There is some ambiguity in the language, chiefly over whether the word for 'controlled' (*dikuasai*) leans towards implying state ownership or simply regulation of natural resources and key production sectors.[119]

However, the scepticism towards foreign business and private capital more generally is clear. As explained by Wilopo, who was prime minister for just over a year during the early 1950s, the family basis of the economy was designed as a deliberate rejection of the Western economic liberalism that had brought 'misery and injustice' to Asian colonies. Indonesia favoured the 'assistance and protection of the state' as opposed to the private sector focus of liberalism.[120] That spirit lives on in Indonesia, from explicit self-sufficiency targets for key foodstuffs, to widespread import restrictions and government price controls for everything from fresh produce to airfares and off-street parking.

Protectionism runs much deeper in Indonesia than many economists like to admit. They tend to argue that Indonesia's economic nationalism is driven by 'Sadli's Law', which states that the bad times make for good policy and the good times make for bad policy.[121] When prices for Indonesia's commodities are high, as during the SBY years, the government is cash-rich and can afford to be picky about foreign investment. By contrast, the argument goes, when commodity prices fall, as happened during Jokowi's time in office, governments should open the economy to make up for the financial shortfall. But Indonesia's history, and Jokowi's track record, demonstrate that social and political attitudes often override the impact of market forces.

*

Indonesia's inconsistent economic policy has been compounded by Jokowi's style of governing on the fly. Several people who worked closely with him explained that the president becomes impatient when listening to detailed arguments. 'Jokowi is instinctive and stubborn,' said one senior official. 'Once he's decided on something it's very hard to change his mind.' SBY was the opposite in many ways. 'He was indecisive, yes. But he'd also listen to advice. He could be swayed by logical arguments either way. And he'd make up his mind based on the facts.'[122]

Another senior official said that working with Jokowi had become harder as he became more entrenched in power. 'Jokowi says what he wants, whatever the consequences,' he said. 'He's not always very subtle.'[123]

The disregard for expert advice – a global theme of our times – became painfully apparent in the early days of the COVID-19 pandemic in 2020. Jokowi played down the threat to Indonesia and refused to disclose information about the spread of the disease, claiming he didn't want to 'panic' the population. Meanwhile, his health minister, a controversial former army doctor, initially suggested Indonesians would be spared by prayer.[124]

As the death toll spiralled, Jokowi tried to block efforts by local leaders to implement much-needed social distancing measures.[125] While he appeared to sideline the epidemiologists, Jokowi put current and former military figures in charge of the response, a move that underlined his view of the crisis as one of internal control as much as health.[126]

The president's defenders argued that he was driven, like many other world leaders, by a desire to ensure that the economic pain of fighting the pandemic was not worse than the disease itself. However, the disarray prompted an outpouring of public criticism from scientists.[127]

Unusually, one of his former senior advisers, Yanuar Nugroho, joined the chorus of concern. He said the government's response to COVID-19 was indecisive and lacking in transparency, risking 'widespread transmission and casualties' as well as a 'collapse of public confidence'. He argued that the pandemic should be a 'wake-up call' to Jokowi to bring expertise and evidence back into policymaking.[128]

For Jokowi's economic team, the sense that he was straying into dangerous territory had crystallised around the time of his decision to build a new capital city, 1300 kilometres across the sea in the forests of East Kalimantan. The dream of creating a dedicated capital – Indonesia's own Brasilia, Canberra, or Naypyidaw – has been floating around since the days of Sukarno, like many other bad ideas in Indonesia. Although Jokowi asked the national planning ministry in 2017 to examine different possible sites outside Java, no-one expected this to be anything other than the usual lip service to something that would never happen.

Indonesian officials are adept at kicking improbable projects into the long grass, from plans to unify the country's three time zones, to proposals to re-denominate the currency so that a bowl of noodles does not cost thousands of rupiah (neither is happening any time soon). But, as Jokowi tried to reassert his authority in the aftermath of the 2019 election when Prabowo was still claiming victory, he suddenly got much more serious about the capital move. He confirmed his plans by August, saying that he wanted construction of the US$33 billion project to start as soon as possible, with the intention that it would be ready by 2024, when his second and final term ends.

Proponents see the new capital as necessary to relieve pressure on Jakarta, which faces growing flood risks on top of its terrible traffic jams and overcrowding. The world's second biggest urban area after Tokyo, Jakarta is sinking into the sea by 12 centimetres a year due to excess groundwater being pumped out as a result of the surging population.[129] Jokowi has also argued that the new capital is needed to spread development beyond the economic powerhouse of Java, and to realise Indonesia's destiny to become an advanced nation.[130]

Other officials have suggested that Jokowi is motivated by a desire to escape from the clutches of Jakarta, a city that, as we shall see in the next chapter, has brought him much political suffering as well as being his bridge to the presidency.[131] He certainly seems enamoured with the symbolism of creating a shiny new capital in his own image, the enduring legacy of the hard-hat president. There is an unmistakable historical parallel, not just with Sukarno and the other presidents who tried and failed to move the capital, but with the most successful historical kingdoms of these islands. They were named for their main cities: Majapahit, Singhasari, Kediri, and Demak.[132]

Jokowi has prioritised development outside Java more than previous Indonesian leaders, seeing it as a way to better balance the economy and redress historic inequalities.[133] Java, which is smaller in size than New Zealand's South Island, is home to more than 150 million people, accounts for 59 per cent of economic activity in Indonesia, and has long dominated the country's politics.[134] Indonesia's outlying provinces are less connected, less wealthy, and often overlooked by politicians in Jakarta.

But Jokopolis, as Indonesians have mockingly dubbed the new capital, is more likely to prove an embarrassment than a crowning glory. Even Jokowi's first-term Vice President, Jusuf Kalla, criticised the plan before stepping down in 2019, arguing that it needed to be 'more thorough'.[135] 'It's okay to relocate the capital but it is a huge undertaking,' he said. 'One has to carefully check the land even when buying a house.'

Economists expect costs to soar way beyond Jokowi's US$33 billion price tag and it is doubtful that private investors will provide much of the cash, as the government hopes. While other developed and developing countries have built new capitals, with varying degrees of success, few have attempted to create a new capital so far from the existing one.

A much more sensible idea would be to put the administrative centre in Java, perhaps along the high-speed rail line now under construction between Jakarta and Bandung, which is backed by Chinese technology and capital. But that would look a bit too much like copying Malaysia, where former Prime Minister Mahathir Mohamad built a new government base outside Kuala Lumpur. That is never a good look in Indonesia, given the longstanding rivalry with its neighbour.

There is a real risk that such a complex but ill-considered project will be badly executed. There are also substantial opportunity costs. There would be many better ways to spend the cash, not least by improving the health system that has been found wanting by COVID-19. One silver lining of the pandemic is that it may prompt Jokowi to reassess or abandon the Jokopolis plans. If he goes ahead, it will not just be a waste of Indonesia's limited financial resources, but also of Jokowi's precious political capital, which he collects jealously but rarely spends.

After six years as president, Jokowi's simplistic approach to the economy seems to have exhausted itself. But, as a political ally told me, one of Jokowi's greatest strengths is 'that people keep underestimating him'.[136] Rather than chasing the capital dream and succumbing to his 'edifice complex', Jokowi should use the aftermath of the pandemic to rethink his economic policy and take advice from experts much more seriously.

While he has struggled to find the middle ground between economic nationalism and the need for foreign investment, there is a better way forward based on a more honest vision for Indonesia. Japan, South Korea, and Taiwan have used smart industrial policy to become wealthy, developed nations, protecting key industries while simultaneously making sure they are internationally competitive. But instead of clarifying his positions over time, Jokowi has tended to lurch from problem to problem, becoming ever more subsumed by the defining contradictions of modern Indonesian history.

CHAPTER FIVE

Between democracy and authoritarianism

On a drizzly Jakarta Friday in December 2016, Jokowi walked out of the presidential palace holding a blue umbrella and dressed in his typical office garb of black trousers and untucked white shirt. But this wasn't going to be just another *blusukan*. The president, who was escorted by then Vice President Jusuf Kalla, police chief Tito Karnavian, and a gaggle of ministers and bodyguards, was wearing a black *peci*, the traditional hat worn by Muslim men, and was on his way to a very unusual Friday prayer meeting.

Just across the road from the palace, hundreds of thousands of conservative and hardline Muslims had gathered at the National Monument. They were there to demand the political defenestration of Basuki Tjahaja Purnama, the governor of Jakarta and one of Jokowi's closest allies.

Ahok, as he was known, was a double minority in the world's most populous Muslim majority nation: ethnically Chinese and a devout Christian. Ahok had run as Jokowi's deputy during the 2012 Jakarta gubernatorial election and had taken over as governor when Jokowi became president in 2014 – a step forward for tolerance in the eyes of Jokowi, who also had a Christian deputy in Solo. Hailed for his uncompromising but effective approach to running the city, Ahok had been well on course to be re-elected the following year, cementing his place as the country's most successful minority leader.

That would have been a breakthrough moment for diversity in Indonesia, which has been battling with more doctrinaire strains of Islam since independence in 1945. But some throwaway remarks Ahok made in September of 2016 sparked a chain reaction that would lead to his downfall and imprisonment, shake Jokowi's leadership to the core, and expose the fragility of democracy in Indonesia. The crisis, and its lingering after-effects, would erode the image of Indonesia as a beacon of democracy and pluralism in the Muslim world, a view promoted by Barack Obama among others.[137]

In a classic demonstration of the chaos effect, the flapping of the butterfly's wings happened when Governor Ahok was on an everyday visit to the

Thousand Islands, a sparse community of fishermen more than 50 kilometres off the coast of Jakarta. Speaking to about 100 locals and officials, he suggested that some people had been 'misled' by Muslims who claimed a well-known verse in the Koran forbade them from voting for non-Muslims like him. It was a sign of his annoyance with the regular but small protests against him organised by hardline groups such as the Islamic Defenders Front (FPI), which doubled as a thuggish gang under the leadership of hot-headed preacher Habib Rizieq Shihab.

Like many of Ahok's outbursts, it was needless. But few who attended the event even noticed it. Without amplification, the comments would almost certainly have disappeared into the flotsam and jetsam of daily news coverage. Instead, his remarks were recorded, edited to seem more incriminating, and uploaded to YouTube.

At first, it was just hardliners who accused Ahok of insulting Muslims, clerics, and the Koran itself – all possible criminal offences under Indonesia's controversial blasphemy law. But then Indonesia's top clerical body, the Indonesian Ulema Council (MUI), stepped into the fray. Some two weeks after the fateful trip to the Thousand Islands, MUI warned Ahok to focus on his job and avoid provocative statements.

A couple of days later, the organisation, which was led by conservative cleric (later to become Jokowi's vice president) Ma'ruf Amin, upped the ante. They issued a 'religious opinion' that Muslims were indeed obliged to vote for Muslims, that those who denied it were defaming the Koran and insulting Muslims, and that they should be punished by the law.[138]

That prompted a series of spiralling protests, which Jokowi's political opponents, including Prabowo, looked to exploit. Prabowo's team had damaged Jokowi's reputation in the eyes of conservative Muslims during the 2014 election by spreading propaganda that falsely claimed he was ethnically Chinese, Christian, and communist.

Now, ahead of the Jakarta gubernatorial election in early 2017 and the presidential election of 2019, they sniffed a chance to further weaken Jokowi by destroying Ahok and helping Prabowo's preferred governor, Anies Baswedan, get elected in Jakarta. Susilo Bambang Yudhoyono, whose eldest son Agus Harimurti Yudhoyono was the third candidate for the Jakarta governorship, also sensed an opportunity to benefit from Ahok and Jokowi's woes.[139]

In the wake of the crisis, analysts would debate whether the anti-Ahok campaign was driven by a grassroots Islamist movement or was the result of elite politicians manipulating the public. As so often in history, it was in fact a combination of deep social forces, high-level machinations, and happenstance.

The backing of leaders like Prabowo and Ma'ruf, who would later testify against Ahok at his blasphemy trial, lent credibility to formerly fringe figures like Habib Rizieq. Tens of thousands attended a mass protest against Ahok in Jakarta on 4 November 2016, which descended into a late-night riot in front of the gates of the presidential palace.[140] That was dwarfed by the next protest, on 2 December, when hundreds of thousands (at a conservative estimate) descended on the capital, blocking off surrounding routes to the large square that contains the National Monument.[141]

In the palace, Jokowi was taken aback by the scale and fervour of the 212 movement, as it was called in reference to the date of the protest. He had already been scarred by the Islamist attacks on him in the 2014 election campaign, saying that the spread of lies about his background made him 'extraordinarily sad'.[142] Some of his team feared that, although pitched as a peaceful prayer session, the protest could turn violent and the palace could easily be overwhelmed by the hordes next door.

In their darkest moments that day, some worried that, if handled badly, this could turn into an Iran-style Islamic Revolution.[143] So Jokowi, umbrella in hand, decided to try to defuse the situation by going to pray on stage with Habib Rizieq and his followers. Taking the microphone himself, Jokowi praised the protesters for their orderly behaviour, interspersing his brief comments with unusual (for him) chants of '*Allahu akbar*' ('God is the greatest').[144]

It was a defining moment for Jokowi. By giving credence to the demands of intolerant hardliners like Habib Rizieq, he had sealed the fate of Ahok, his friend and colleague. He had also legitimised a radical movement that would be a thorn in his side for years to come, and empowered his chief rival, Prabowo, on the national stage. But he succeeded in easing the tensions, and most of the massed protesters went home that evening by the same legion of busses that had brought them. To Jokowi's supporters, it was a classic example of him using the Javanese approach to politics, *menang tanpa ngasorake*, or 'winning without humiliating your adversary'.[145]

If Jokowi won that day, it was a defeat for democracy and pluralism in Indonesia. While Indonesia's courts are meant to be independent of the executive, and impervious to public pressure, Jokowi's appearance at the rally made it almost inevitable that Ahok would be convicted. The credence Jokowi lent to the anti-Ahok movement helped further weaken the governor's popularity, which had been very high before September.

Ahok eventually lost the run-off election to Anies Baswedan in April 2017, after none of the three candidates secured the required vote share of more than 50 per cent in the first-round election in February. A month after Anies' victory, Ahok's downfall was complete when he was sentenced to two years in jail for blasphemy. But there was much more at stake than the fate of one man.

Shaken by the power and speed of the 212 movement, Jokowi embarked on what has been called an 'authoritarian turn'.[146] His government sought to legitimise and co-opt certain conservative Islamic groups and individuals while throwing the coercive power of the state at others, tactics redolent of Suharto's New Order government.[147] He used a presidential decree to outlaw Hizbut Tahrir Indonesia, a radical Islamic organisation, while letting Habib Rizieq's more violent FPI roam free, in what one expert called a politically motivated 'abuse of power'.[148]

Then, on the eve of nomination day, Jokowi abandoned his original choice for vice president in 2019,

Mahfud MD, opting for none other than Ma'ruf Amin, the cleric who had precipitated Ahok's demise. Meanwhile, the police and other state bodies were deployed to target Jokowi's critics on an increasingly systematic basis. And the embattled president surrounded himself ever more closely with figures from the military, who sought security-led responses to everything from religious tensions to COVID-19.

Jokowi's inclination towards the military predated the 212 movement. It reflected both the abiding power of the armed forces in Indonesia and the president's desire to use them as a balancing force against his various political opponents.[149] As one officer in the Tentara Nasional Indonesia (TNI), the armed forces, explained in 2015: 'Jokowi is clean and humble, but he's weak and he doesn't have backup from elsewhere in the system – that's why he turns to the army.'[150]

By his second term, Jokowi had brought a praetorian guard of former military figures into his inner circle. There was Luhut of course, in charge of everything from maritime affairs to overseeing the cabinet. Then there was Moeldoko, his chief of staff and a former head of the TNI, as well as Defence Minister Prabowo, Religious Affairs Minister Fachrul Razi, Health Minister Terawan and, lastly, Wiranto, the head of the presidential advisory council. It is important to understand that, unlike in many Western nations, even former senior officers in Indonesia can command significant loyalty from those still serving.

The president's use of these top military men was mirrored by a growing reliance on the TNI to help execute domestic policy at ground level. The military was tasked with an expanding range of objectives that would normally fall within the remit of the civilian administration including, to name a few, distributing fertiliser, helping boost rice production, and testing the quality of coal for power stations.[151] The TNI had been angling to get more influence ever since its *dwifungsi*, or 'dual function', role in civil and military affairs was dismantled after the fall of Suharto.

Jokowi was not intentionally seeking to revive New Order governance structures. Rather, he was reaching for any practical levers of power that might help him achieve his aims. But, regardless of his intentions, the former mayor who used democratisation to rise to the presidency has proven to be a poor guardian of democracy.

The decline in democratic governance extends to the all-important fight against corruption. Having built his early career on his reputation for clean politics, Jokowi has overseen a concerted weakening of the Corruption Eradication Commission (KPK), Indonesia's respected anti-graft agency. He has been cheered on by parliamentarians who have been desperate to destroy the agency for years.

In September 2019, the Dewan Perwakilan Rakyat (DPR) rushed through amendments to the KPK law that significantly diluted the agency's independent investigatory powers.[152] Under fire from legal experts, Jokowi initially suggested he might use his presidential prerogative to overrule the DPR. But he soon backed away from a fight with the parliament and let the controversial amendments stand.[153]

By the start of his second term, activists were calling for his Bung Hatta anti-corruption award to be revoked and students were protesting en masse under the slogan *'reformasi* has been corrupted'.[154] *Tempo*, one of Jokowi's early cheerleaders, argued in an editorial that the president had overseen the 'end of the KPK'. It said that his administration and the DPR bore responsibility 'for the betrayal of those who fought for Indonesian reforms in 1998'.[155]

Many activists were equally despondent. One friend who ran a leading NGO told me that the problem was less Jokowi going rogue than a failure to understand what really made him tick. 'Jokowi cares about corruption as an obstacle to business more than a political principle,' he said. 'He also knows that a strong KPK is a risk to political parties and law enforcement officers, and he knows he needs their support to deliver his economic programs.'[156]

This pragmatic Jokowi had been busy amassing support from the sorts of political parties, businesspeople, and media owners who had often been targeted by the KPK. Some appeared to have been nudged, such as Hary Tanoesoedibjo, a brash tycoon and business partner of Donald Trump who had been one of Jokowi's staunchest critics. Hary switched his support to Jokowi in 2017 after he was charged with threatening a public prosecutor, a case that has not progressed since. His influential media outlets became much more supportive of the president and Hary was rewarded after the election when his daughter was made deputy minister for tourism at the age of 32.[157]

Others turned towards Jokowi of their own volition when they saw that he was likely to win re-election in 2019. The result was that the largely tycoon-controlled media, with allegiances divided between Prabowo and Jokowi in 2014, became almost uniformly pro-Jokowi. It was a perfect demonstration of the lack of ideology and the power of patronage in Indonesian political life. As Jeffrey Winters, an American professor who literally wrote the book on oligarchy in Indonesia, once told me, the elite will ultimately 'line up like ducks in a row' behind whoever is accumulating the most power.[158]

The most belated, and unexpected, duck to fall into line was Prabowo Subianto himself. Despite the dirtiest campaign Indonesia had seen for years, with both camps firing online disinformation at the other, Jokowi won the 2019 election by a slightly larger margin than in 2014, with 55.5 per cent of the vote to Prabowo's 45.5 per cent. It was the fourth time Prabowo had failed to reach the apex of power in an electoral process. As well as the 2014 and 2019 elections, he had also fallen short in Golkar's convention to select a presidential candidate in 2004 and lost alongside Megawati as her would-be vice president in 2009.

The 2019 loss was a bitter blow for the ever-ambitious 69-year-old former general, who had once told me he was not so much 'born to rule' but 'born to serve'. He was the son and grandson of revolutionary national heroes, and a descendent of the last Javanese sultan to hold out against the Dutch invasion.[159] The CIA seemed to agree with Prabowo's view of his own trajectory. Two years after he married one of Suharto's daughters in 1983, CIA analysts picked out the then 32-year-old Prabowo as a 'future dark horse' to succeed his father-in-law.[160] But Indonesian voters were evidently less keen.

Prabowo, a complicated man whose fiery temper was matched by his erudition, did not take his final defeat by Jokowi well. He claimed, with minimal evidence, that the election had been stolen from him, just as he had done in 2009 and 2014, before eventually accepting the result months later, after lengthy legal challenges.

This time, with his hardline supporters triggered by a highly polarised campaign, the anger spilt over into deadly riots on the streets of Jakarta in May 2019. The outbreak of violence prompted the government to restrict the use of WhatsApp and other social media platforms for the first time in Indonesian history.[161]

Allegations flew around Jakarta about whether the clashes were organic, or had been orchestrated by Prabowo's team, or even people close to the government. With the police having become progressively politicised, it was hard to know who to believe. But Prabowo soon backed off, as expected. Just two months later, the great reconciliation took place, another example of Jokowi 'winning without humiliating'.

Jokowi chose to meet his long-time rival on the recently opened Jakarta metro, a not-so-subtle symbol that he was the guy who got things done while Prabowo was, well, Prabowo.[162] Rather than finish the rapprochement with a photo opportunity, Jokowi went a step further, appointing Prabowo as defence minister in October. It was the first time Prabowo had held public office since his ignominious fall from the military, and self-exile overseas, in the wake of Suharto's ouster.

Prabowo's comeback was symptomatic of the topsy-turvy nature of Indonesian politics. It represented a remarkable reunion of the original political triumvirate that had propelled Jokowi onto the national stage, when Megawati and Prabowo backed him to run as Jakarta governor in 2012.

The former general was not a man to bear a grudge lightly. When I visited his hilltop ranch outside Jakarta in 2013, he told me that he could 'count on the fingers of one hand' the number of people in his life who had never betrayed him. At a later lunch in the Four Seasons Hotel, he expanded on his dark view of humanity, contrasting it with his affection for animals. 'When we grow up and see human nature, there's betrayal, perfidy, lying,' he said. 'But some of these animals are very basic. You give love to them, they give love back. You are loyal to them. They are loyal to you.'[163]

Prabowo and his tycoon brother, Hashim Djojohadikusumo, had provided crucial funding for

Jokowi's campaign for Jakarta governor in 2012. And they were bitterly disappointed when Jokowi used his new platform to snatch the presidency from Prabowo's grasp.

But Prabowo's return wasn't just a political psychodrama. It was, for many true believers in Jokowi's transformative potential, the final straw. Part of the problem was that Jokowi had put in charge of the military a former general accused of human rights abuses who had previously been banned from entering the United States as a result.

The bigger issue was that the move seemed to undermine the point of democracy itself. Why had Jokowi fought two intense, and at times nasty, election campaigns against Prabowo only to bring him to power later? And with Jokowi's coalition now expanded to nearly three quarters of the DPR, who would provide something resembling opposition, which is a *sine qua non* for real democracy? 'The moment he picked Prabowo in his cabinet was the end for me,' one official told me. 'He did it to neutralise opposition, not out of true strength.'

Academics and journalists have tended to see this depressing picture as part of a global decline in democracy – from Rodrigo Duterte in the Philippines and Viktor Orbán in Hungary, to Jair Bolsonaro in Brazil and Donald Trump in the United States. But while there is an undeniable international trend, the direction of travel in Indonesia is overwhelmingly being driven by domestic factors.

Unusually, Indonesia has continued to enjoy resilient, free, and fair elections while democratic principles have eroded over the last few years. The pressure on democracy has increased and become more worrying under Jokowi. But it predates him. In particular, the growing appeasement of conservative Islamic figures and the increasing intolerance and violence towards religious minorities and the LGBT community can be traced back to the SBY years.[164]

More broadly, *reformasi* ran out of steam after the successful early efforts at democratisation and decentralisation. The result is that Indonesian politics, the bureaucracy, and the military remain full of people whose commitment to democracy runs only skin deep. Authoritarianism in Indonesia never truly went away. At the same time, there is a deep historical scepticism towards Western-style liberal democracy, just as there is towards its close relative, economic liberalism.

Tension over the role of Islam in the Indonesian state also dates to the years of Indonesia's foundation. The pluralist Sukarno reached a compromise with Islamists who wanted Shariah law by making Indonesia a religious state, where belief in God was compulsory but there was a choice of six official religions. Indonesia occupies a unique position in the Muslim world, not secular, but not an Islamic state like Brunei or Pakistan. Yet, the necessarily messy compromise of 1945 has not held fast, and it has been tested ever since by a series of rebellions and popular movements.

The broader struggle between orthodox Muslims and the *abangan*, who like Jokowi himself blend Islam with traditional Javanese beliefs, dates back much further than 1945. Atmodarminto, a delegate to the Constitutional Assembly that debated the role of Islam in the state from 1956 to 1959, hoped that this long-running religious conflict would finally be resolved by an independent Indonesia.[165] However, his warning that the struggle tends to be provoked or exacerbated by 'power-seeking leaders' proved more prophetic than his wish for resolution.

The simultaneous legislative and presidential elections in 2019 offered uncanny echoes of the religious divides of the 1955 legislative election.[166] One camp of voters, which lined up behind Jokowi, was composed of *abangan* Muslims in Central and East Java together with religious minority groups in outlying areas such as Bali and Papua. Overall, Jokowi won 97 per cent of non-Muslim votes.[167] The other camp, which lined up behind Prabowo, incorporated parts of Indonesia that lean towards more orthodox Islam including West Java, West Sumatra, and South Sulawesi.[168]

If Indonesia is still suffering the growing pains of a young nation, why does Jokowi get so much blame for Indonesia's democratic decline? One important reason is because activists and analysts placed so much hope in him before the 2014 election. Frustrated with the inaction of the SBY years and rightly fearful of the consequences for democracy of a Prabowo victory, they looked to Jokowi as the only alternative. The then Jakarta governor played up these expectations, happy to egg on his enthusiastic supporters. In his 2014 manifesto, Jokowi promised to reform the legal system, promote clean democratic governance, uphold human rights, and investigate past human rights abuses. But these were formulaic statements rather than commitments to meaningful action.

Jokowi seems to view democracy largely as a way to achieve his desired economic outcomes. In late 2013, a year after he had become Jakarta governor, I sat down with him in City Hall to see how he was finding the new job and explore his political thinking as speculation swirled that he would run for the presidency.

A few months earlier, a new museum had opened in Suharto's birth village of Kemusuk, less than 100 kilometres from where Jokowi was born in Central Java. The museum paid tribute to the life and work of the long-ruling autocrat and his kleptocratic family. It attracted a lot of interest, symbolising a growing exasperation with the intricacies of democracy. There was a popular sense that life was easier under Suharto 'because you only had to pay one person off back then'.

Was Jokowi convinced that democracy was the right system for Indonesia? 'Democracy is about improving the lives of the people,' he responded, before he repeated his standard line about asking the people what they want and finding practical solutions.[169] I wondered if he was being deliberately evasive but, looking at his track record, it seems that he really does see democracy in such functional terms. If it brings society together and expands the economy, then it's a good thing. But it's the means, not the end.

Jokowi's view of democracy as a tool for development seems to align with how many Indonesians see their country. A recent survey found that most Indonesian voters believe democracy is the right political system, but they conceive of it as a 'means of delivering social and economic benefits' rather than upholding rights and civil liberties.[170] This illiberal view of politics is discomforting for the many Indonesia-watchers who want the country to be a democratic success story. However, it is better to acknowledge this complex reality than to harbour unrealistic expectations of democratic transformation, or unfounded fears of a full return to authoritarian rule.

In a revealing comment at the height of the anti-Ahok campaign, Jokowi argued that 'our democracy has gone too far' because it was allowing too much political extremism. By extremism, he meant not just terrorism and sectarianism, but also liberalism.[171] Many of Jokowi's actions have, indeed, been decidedly illiberal. When he was under immense political pressure in the first few months of his presidency, he authorised a spate of executions of convicted drug traffickers as part of a securitised war on drugs, which experts said was 'doing more harm than good'.[172]

On tolerance and pluralism, Jokowi said the right things and spent much more time visiting outlying minority areas than his predecessors. But he has been unwilling to spend his political capital to defend minority rights. In Papua, where a long-running independence struggle has simmered for decades, Jokowi made some positive initial noises, freeing political prisoners and pledging to work harder on human rights.

But, despite regular trips to Papua, his policy is ultimately an extension of previous, ineffective efforts to use security forces to crush the separatist rebels while trying to win over the rest of the population with development projects. Without any effort to engage in dialogue about the fundamental problems of disenfranchisement and systematic violence against the people of Papua, this approach has inevitably failed to cool tensions.[173]

When a new round of deadly clashes erupted in Papua in September 2019, Jokowi's government not only sent in the troops but also, for the first time, completely cut off internet access in the affected areas.[174] It was part of an increasingly draconian crackdown on information and criticism, which was matched by a growing use of state-linked disinformation campaigns.

An independent investigation uncovered one sophisticated and well-funded campaign using automated social media accounts, or 'bots', to flood Facebook and Twitter with pro-Indonesian government views on Papua.[175] It was an intensification of tactics that had become widespread during the 2019 election. Both Jokowi's supporters, and Prabowo's backers, employed teams of paid social media posters, known as 'buzzers', to pump out propaganda and mount vicious attacks on each other.[176]

The government responded by attempting to suppress what it called 'hoax news', but the police were far from even-handed. It was predominantly critics of Jokowi who were arrested under Indonesia's electronic information and transactions law, and other laws that give the authorities wide-ranging powers to police speech.[177] Although some human rights campaigners had hoped that the squeeze would ease after Jokowi's election victory, the push for information control has, in fact, intensified.

As COVID-19 began to spread in Indonesia during early 2020, the police announced that they would target not only those spreading misinformation about the novel coronavirus, but also those who had 'insulted' the president or other government officials.[178] Dozens had already been arrested by that point, many for spreading false rumours about the virus, but some simply for criticising the government.[179]

This increasingly oppressive response reflects the knee-jerk authoritarianism of many senior officials, especially but not exclusively those with a military background. Many current and former TNI officers are steeped in a culture of 'proxy warfare'. They see the main threat to Indonesia as unnamed outside forces using campaigns for more democracy and human rights to sow internal divisions and ultimately destroy the state.[180] As a result, they struggle to see the difference between legitimate government criticism and attempts to destabilise the nation.

The TNI's paranoid fears echo the language of the Communist Parties of China and Vietnam, whose officials constantly warn of plots by 'hostile foreign forces'. It is perhaps a curious analogy, given that Communism and Marxism–Leninism remain illegal in Indonesia, another legacy of the Suharto era. But shared anxiety about outside meddling can create unlikely affinities.

That was apparent when Moeldoko, Jokowi's chief of staff and the former TNI chief, met the Chinese ambassador to Indonesia in late 2019.[181] As the Western world lambasted Beijing's suppression of the Uighur people in Xinjiang, Moeldoko expressed sympathy not for his fellow Muslims, but for the Chinese government. The Indonesian government also found it 'difficult to deal with hoax attacks', he said.

The desire to control the flow of information more tightly is shared widely across the government.

Internet restrictions are likely to be rolled out more frequently, after Jokowi's administration escalated from partial social media controls during the post-election riots in Jakarta in May 2019, to a full internet shutdown in parts of Papua in September.

Johnny Plate, the communications minister in Jokowi's second term and a former businessman, argued that internet shutdowns and other restrictions were necessary to prevent chaos. 'If we are faced with the choice between the state and democracy, we must choose the state,' he said. 'Without the state, democracy is useless.'[182]

The rising tide of authoritarian actions and authoritarian thinking in Jokowi's government has prompted a growing number of people to criticise him as a latter-day Suharto lite.[183] The irony, according to one official, is that he might privately view these comparisons as a tribute to his increasingly strong-willed leadership and his prioritisation of economic development.[184]

Both Jokowi and Suharto came from hard-scrabble beginnings in Central Java, an experience that gave them the toughness and resilience they needed to make their own way to the top of politics. Their backgrounds helped them connect with ordinary Indonesians, without the rhetorical flourishes of most politicians.

They showed little interest in abstract ideas or theorising, and each became president without showing much overt ambition or enthusiasm for the machinations of elite politics. Once installed in the palace, both men developed a harder edge, showing a reluctance to follow advice, while relying on a small circle of acolytes.[185]

Jokowi and Suharto both kept their true feelings about people and power close to their chest, preferring to hide behind the ambiguity of Javanese aphorisms. Several days after Jokowi's kiss-and-make-up session with Prabowo on the new metro, for example, the president tweeted out the Javanese expression *lamun sira sekti, aja mateni*.[186] It roughly translates as 'even though you are powerful, don't knock down others'.

Suharto's biographer could well have been writing of Jokowi when he spoke of 'a mind uncluttered by the problematic or the unresolved, one based on inner reflection on life's personal experiences rather than the ideas of others, and underpinned by a very strongly felt sense of fate, duty and destiny'.[187] Both men believed that their foremost duty was to grow the economy, and development was their 'leitmotiv'.[188]

There are, of course, limits to the comparison. Jokowi's democratic path to the presidency could not have been more different to Suharto's. His formative experience as a small businessman contrasts with Suharto's military career. And, although he seems to be starting a political dynasty of his own and eroding the fight against corruption, Jokowi remains a far cleaner politician than Suharto. He also operates in an Indonesia boasting free and fair elections and many more rights and accountability mechanisms than in the New Order era.

But the parallels with Suharto's rule, and Indonesia's longer struggle between democracy and authoritarianism, are hard to ignore. After he came under attack for bringing Prabowo into the government, Jokowi hit back by insisting there was 'no such thing as opposition in Indonesia'. 'Our democracy is a *gotong royong* democracy,' he said, citing the Indonesian concept of mutual assistance and reflecting the New Order view of 'opposition' as a dirty word.[189]

Jokowi was also echoing Indonesia's founders. Mohammad Hatta had argued that Western liberal democratic traditions were not appropriate for Indonesia because they were too 'individualist', while Indonesian society was fundamentally 'collectivist in nature'.[190] Sukarno, too, insisted that *gotong royong* should be the root of the Indonesian political system.

But is Jokowi really wedded to these views, or merely looking for convenient excuses for his actions? In truth, he has never had a political philosophy. He has been guided by his experience. First, as a factory owner building a small business through the Suharto era into the early years of democratisation, and then as a city mayor with a practical role and practical view of the world. Thrust suddenly onto the national stage, power has revealed a man with surprisingly little to say about the big questions of modern Indonesian history.

Jokowi has never been the democratic reformer that he has allowed some of his boosters to think he is. But neither is he some sort of authoritarian wolf in sheep's clothing. Rather, he has been shaped by the winds that swirl around him. The mass Islamic movement that swept away his key ally Ahok, and the associated smear campaigns against him, blew him off course. He responded by reaching for the guide ropes of authoritarian rule, many of which had been left in place since the fall of Suharto.

Jokowi embodied the hope of Indonesian democracy, where the little man can rise to the top by virtue of hard, honest work. Other local leaders have looked to emulate his early success, listening more to voters, improving basic services, and reducing bureaucracy and corruption. Some are being touted as future national leaders themselves, including Anies Baswedan, the current Governor of Jakarta, Ridwan Kamil, the Governor of West Java, and Khofifah Indar Parawansa, the Governor of East Java.

But now, Jokowi's government is threatening to pull up the ladder by which he reached the top. It is proposing the abolition of direct elections for local leaders and a roll-back of decentralisation.[191] Tito Karnavian, Jokowi's home affairs minister and a former national police chief, has argued that the coming elections are too expensive, pushing candidates to embrace corruption to recoup their campaign costs. He believes, moreover, that voters in some areas are not 'mature' enough for democracy.[192]

Senior figures from established political parties, including the Indonesian Democratic Party of Struggle (PDI-P), have long pushed for direct elections to be abandoned wholesale, a move that would give legislators the power to choose local leaders, and even the president.[193] Jokowi has said he will not support such efforts but, given the way he allowed political parties to weaken the KPK, activists are right to be concerned.

The president, who has grown increasingly perturbed by local leaders defying the national government, has made other moves to strengthen central control. A new high-profile bill on job creation is expected to weaken local government powers over development planning and other areas.[194] And, during the COVID-19 crisis, Jokowi's government tried to stop local leaders from initiating their own lockdown measures to reduce the spread of the coronavirus.[195]

Like Indonesia, Jokowi seems stuck between democracy and authoritarianism. However much he wants to remake Indonesia, and however much activists wish to see a more democratic nation, hope alone is not enough to overcome the heavy burden of history.

CHAPTER SIX

Jokowi and the world: From Asia's new fulcrum to friends with benefits

As the path to the presidency opened in 2013 and 2014, Jokowi showed little interest in foreign policy beyond a knack for charming the international correspondents and investors that he believed could boost his image and promote economic growth. However, as he approached his debut on the international political stage at the East Asia Summit in Myanmar in November 2014, his foreign policy advisers were eager for him to make a splash.

Led by Rizal Sukma, who ran the country's leading think tank and would later be rewarded with the ambassadorship to the United Kingdom, they had come up with the idea of turning Indonesia into a 'global maritime fulcrum'. Jokowi duly unveiled this rather woolly concept in Naypyidaw, Myanmar's bizarre and empty purpose-built capital, to an audience of world leaders, including Barack Obama, Dmitry Medvedev, Li Keqiang, and Shinzo Abe.[196]

The idea would later be exalted by foreign governments from the United States to China as a kind of manifesto for Indonesia to play a much bigger role in the increasingly thorny diplomacy of the region.[197] But it was, like so many political speeches, heavy on buzzwords, thin on policy, and designed to be all things to all people.

Most of the 'five pillars' of the fulcrum were about domestic policy and the economy: promoting the fishing industry, building maritime infrastructure, and defending Indonesia's sovereignty at a time of intensifying territorial disputes. Jokowi did mention the need for 'maritime diplomacy' and international cooperation to reduce the risk of conflict in the South China Sea and beyond. But the concept was not fleshed out. And the president rarely spoke about it again, not even mentioning foreign policy or maritime issues in his second-term inauguration speech in 2019.[198]

Foreign governments have repeatedly placed far too much hope in Jokowi's ability to step up in the global arena. A more careful examination of his views and habits would have left them disabused of that notion. Just days after the new president gave the maritime fulcrum speech, he divulged his real feelings about foreign policy on the flight back to Jakarta. 'For me "free and active" is making friends with countries that can provide us with benefits,' he said. 'What's the point of making friends if we are always on the losing end?'[199]

Jokowi was referring to the founding principle of Indonesia's engagement with the world, that it should be 'free and active' or *bebas dan aktif*. That meant, chiefly, no formal military or security alliances with other nations. He was also implicitly criticising the approach of his predecessor, Susilo Bambang Yudhoyono, who adopted a policy of 'a thousand friends and no enemies' or 'a million friends and no enemies', depending on how affable he was feeling.[200] Thin-skinned and vain, SBY had sought acclaim in the theatre of diplomacy. A fluent English speaker, he was genuinely interested in trying to make Indonesia influential on the global stage, assisted by his eloquent and high-profile foreign ministers, Marty Natalegawa and Hassan Wirajuda.[201]

Jokowi, by contrast, disliked the formalities of diplomacy and public speaking. More importantly, he thought that, just as with democracy, foreign policy should be put to work to boost his overriding obsessions: the economy, infrastructure, and his personal bank of political capital.

Fittingly, Jokowi's ghostwritten autobiography contains only a short chapter on foreign policy. It mostly consists of photographs of him gladhanding world leaders. In the brief text, Jokowi sounds more like a furniture exporter than a disciple of Sukarno, Metternich, or Kissinger, talking of the need to 'boost quality Indonesian products, reduce our dependency on imports, create balance, and expand the scope of export markets'.[202]

Although he has taken Indonesia down a slightly more unilateral path, Jokowi is driven by instinct, whim, and the winds of fortune. He has no strong sense of where he wants Indonesia to go. He vacillates often. Sometimes he tells international audiences what they want to hear about opening Indonesia's markets and supporting globalisation, using references to *The Avengers* and *Game of Thrones*.[203]

Recently, he has shown a renewed enthusiasm for bilateral trade agreements, signing one with Australia in early 2020 after years of arduous negotiations.[204] Yet, it is hardly part of a broader strategy to embrace free trade. When talking to domestic audiences, he usually shows his nationalistic streak, repeating Sukarno's calls for Indonesia to 'stand on its own feet'.[205]

As with his domestic economic policy and his approach to democracy, Jokowi's stance reflects the contradictions of Indonesia's post-independence history. Like Suharto, he wants to use foreign policy as a tool to generate investment. That often conflicts with the perceived need to preserve national dignity and limit outside interference in Indonesia's internal affairs – an ever-present, and rarely justified, fear for the military. The outcome is an Indonesia that confounds: a far-flung archipelagic state that is protectionist in nature despite its rich ancient history of trading links and its strategic location along key global shipping routes.[206]

Jokowi's foreign policy has always been unpredictable, seesawing between nationalism and globalism. At times, he has demonstrated a steeliness that took outsiders by surprise. In 2015, Jokowi authorised the execution of more than a dozen drug traffickers, many of whom were foreign citizens, despite concerns about the impact on international relations. Australia even withdrew its ambassador after Jokowi signed off on two of its citizens being put in front of the firing squad. Jokowi pushed ahead, confident that his tough approach was popular at home. However, he later followed SBY's lead in implementing an unofficial moratorium on executions to stem the outside pressure he was generating.[207]

The president took a similar scattergun approach to the maritime disputes that have increasingly troubled Indonesia. As China escalated its struggle with its Southeast Asian neighbours for control of the region's rich fishing grounds and reserves of oil and gas, there were some initial signs that Jokowi would take a more resolute stance.[208] But he was driven by evolving events, rather than seeking to control them. His responses were ineffective, targeted at maximising media attention rather than achieving concrete results.

The hallmark maritime policy of his first term was the theatrical blowing-up of some of the many foreign fishing boats that crossed into Indonesia's sprawling exclusive economic zone. This incredibly popular measure was the brainchild of his then fisheries minister Susi Pudjiastuti. A high school dropout who had built successful aviation and seafood businesses, she seemed to embody a public desire for decisive leadership that contrasted with Jokowi's Javanese-style 'winning without humiliating'. However, it was not an effective way to police Indonesia's waters. Southeast Asian neighbours, such as Vietnam, suffered the brunt of the policy while bigger, better-equipped Chinese boats tended to evade capture and retribution.

Likewise, when Chinese encroachment into

Indonesia's fishing grounds led to tense incidents involving the Indonesian Coast Guard and Navy in 2016 and 2020, Jokowi's response was more symbolic than substantive. Both times he flew out to the Natuna Islands, near the disputed waters at the southern tip of the South China Sea, and asserted his willingness to defend Indonesian sovereignty.[209]

His government also made several other moves to signal its intent to protect Indonesian waters during his first term. In late 2014, it established a new agency called Bakamla, which was meant to coordinate the country's various and overlapping coast guard–like services. In 2017, it started calling the parts of the South China Sea that fall within Indonesia's exclusive economic zone the 'North Natuna Sea', echoing a similar naming shift by the Philippines.[210] And in 2018, Indonesia opened a new military base on the largest of the Natuna Islands.[211] But these responses were disjointed and, despite the occasional tough talk, there was no concerted improvement in Indonesia's maritime capability or coordination.[212]

On the wider diplomatic stage, Jokowi was limited in his impact, by design. He chose a foreign minister, Retno Marsudi, who had a lower profile than her SBY-era predecessors. Officials from other Southeast Asian nations have subsequently noted that, under

Jokowi's leadership, Indonesia has taken a less active role in regional forums.[213]

The occasional signs of assertion in the South China Sea and on other issues have not been matched by sustained efforts to work more closely with neighbours in pushing back against pressure from Beijing.[214] When the Philippines in 2016 won a landmark legal ruling against China's 'nine-dash line' – its claim to the resources of much of the South China Sea – Indonesia's response was muted.[215] 'Why should we risk upsetting China by vocally supporting the Philippines?' one senior diplomat asked me. 'This way, we get all the benefits of the ruling, with none of the downside.'[216]

While Indonesia coasted, the contours of power in Asia were shifting dramatically around it. Xi Jinping had torn up former paramount leader Deng Xiaoping's advice that China should 'hide its strength and bide its time'. He was taking an ever more muscular approach, with the goal of building a hegemonic position for Beijing in the region. Donald Trump had responded with a chaotic 'America First' approach that, on one hand, meant more bullying and cajoling from Washington but, on the other, raised the fear of American abandonment.

Indonesia's Southeast Asian neighbours, meanwhile, were mostly turning inwards as they too faced intractable domestic problems. The best Indonesia could do was to push ASEAN to issue a fuzzy statement that criticised the 'deepening of mistrust, miscalculation, and patterns of behaviour based on a zero-sum game'.[217] The ASEAN Outlook on the Indo–Pacific, which was adopted in 2019, was little more than a restatement of ASEAN's main principles: peaceful settlement of disputes, respect for international law and, most importantly, non-interference in other nations' internal affairs.

Diplomats from Malaysia, Singapore, and other ASEAN neighbours were bemused by Indonesia's enthusiastic efforts to promote an idea that was so thin. That was why they insisted on calling it an 'outlook' rather than a policy or a strategy.[218] However, that did not prevent Western nations including the United States and Australia from erroneously framing it as a signal of Indonesian intent to stand up in the world, just as they had done with the global maritime fulcrum.

Jokowi's ad hoc leadership style exacerbates the weaknesses of Indonesian foreign policy. He has cancelled several foreign trips at late notice because of domestic political difficulties and, when he does go overseas, he can be a temperamental traveller.

Sometimes he gels with his counterparts and ignores his formal talking points, and at other times he reads out speeches in robotic fashion.[219]

The president also has a tendency to make ill-considered statements, prompting a flurry of misplaced excitement from foreign diplomats. On a visit to the White House in 2015, Jokowi told President Obama that Indonesia would join the Trans-Pacific Partnership (TPP), a potentially landmark trade agreement from which Trump later retreated. The announcement was seen as a diplomatic coup for the Obama administration.[220] But when Jokowi was inevitably criticised at home for threatening to flood Indonesia with imports, he backed away. Indonesia is not currently negotiating to join the agreement that superseded the TPP.

Just a few months before the US visit in 2015, Jokowi had been on the attack against US-led economic institutions and the 'global injustice' he said they represented. At a conference to commemorate the 60th anniversary of Sukarno's Asian–African Conference in Bandung, he called for a 'new global economic order' to replace the Washington-dominated World Bank and International Monetary Fund (IMF).[221] Yet, despite his Sukarno-esque rhetoric, Jokowi's government continued to rely heavily on advice and funding from the IMF and World Bank.

As with Jokowi's economic policy, in the absence of a strategy, personalised rule can only take foreign policy so far. That point was driven home to me by a friend and long-time Jakarta resident who advised foreign companies investing in Indonesia.

One of his clients, the chief executive of a major US corporation, had secured a one-on-one meeting with Jokowi to discuss the interminable problems his company had experienced in obtaining government permits. 'It was incredible to sit there with the president, with no advisers present, and have him listen directly to my concerns,' the chief executive related. But, my friend pointed out, with no note-takers in the room and no policy implementation unit in the palace, who was going to follow up?

If Jokowi wants friends with benefits – what economists would call mercantilism – he has no real plan to win them over, beyond his personal charm and a rotating cast of supporting officials. At the start of his second term, Jokowi appointed Mahendra Siregar, a respected diplomat and former finance official, as deputy foreign minister, with a specific focus on economic diplomacy.[222] But, at the same time, he replaced Tom Lembong, an effective salesman for Indonesia in global financial markets, with a low-profile figure as the head of the investment promotion board.

Meanwhile, Jokowi transferred formal responsibility for generating investment from the coordinating ministry for economic affairs to the coordinating ministry for maritime affairs, led by his fixer-in-chief Luhut.[223] Luhut would become an ever more regular presence on Jokowi's foreign trips. He also began conducting his own diplomacy, developing a relationship with Jared Kushner, Trump's son-in-law and consigliere, as he sought to attract investment from the United States into the planned new capital in Kalimantan.[224]

It seemed more like a game of whack-a-mole than a proper plan. In early 2020, as the economy showed signs of weakness while still chugging along at 5 per cent growth, Jokowi asked his ambassadors to put '70–80 per cent' of their focus on economic diplomacy.[225] It was a genuine reflection of how he sees the world. But, as several diplomats complained to me, there was little meat on the bones of his statement. 'We are not set up to manage our foreign policy that way,' one disaffected official told me. 'We don't have the training to do that.'

As he tried to push the foreign ministry in a new direction, Jokowi had little regard for the traditional diplomatic showpieces. In his first five years, Jokowi didn't attend a single UN General Assembly, which is a firm fixture on the calendar for most world leaders, sending Vice President Jusuf Kalla in his place. 'Jokowi's view would be, why do I have to go to the United Nations, there's no money there and in fact we have to pay them,' one senior official in Jakarta explained to me. 'Instead, he prefers going to the G20 and APEC because they are all about boosting trade and investment.' Like other aspects of his leadership, the official added, 'Jokowi's all about the practicalities, he's just not interested in concepts.'

Jokowi has been smart in using his personal appeal to burnish Indonesia's image in the international economic arena. It is not a substitute for much-needed economic reforms or a consistent trade policy, but it has no doubt helped the country maintain a decent flow of foreign investment and lending, allowing it to sustain growth and cover the annual budget deficits.

Even though economists were squirming over his plans to build a new capital city, Jokowi managed to bring in a slate of high-profile foreign advisers for the project, including former UK Prime Minister Tony Blair, Masayoshi Son, the head of Japanese tech investment group SoftBank, and Sheikh Mohammed bin Zayed Al Nahyan, the crown prince of oil-rich Abu Dhabi.[226]

They are not necessarily going to invest in the project themselves, but they generate attention and give what is a questionable plan a veneer of credibility. His English-language speeches at global business forums, while rarely fluent, have also bolstered the sense that he is a 'can-do' leader.[227] Repeating calls for economic reform might not make it happen, but it does seem to help spread a positive narrative in the influential international financial press.

Jokowi's approach to the outside world has been shaped by history, as much as his idiosyncrasies. Indonesia's 'free and active' stance has not remained static in its execution, shifting with the tides of time and the currents of leadership. In the fragile early days after independence, Sukarno tried to stay on good terms with both the emerging Eastern and Western blocs.

However, once he had seized power in the Guided Democracy era, Sukarno became more erratic in his behaviour and yet more targeted in his diplomacy. He increasingly sided with what he called the New Emerging Forces, proud post-colonial nations, against the Old Established Forces of imperialism. This meant pulling out of the United Nations, moving closer to China, and sparking *Konfrontasi* with a newly independent Malaysia, which Sukarno feared was part of a British plot to contain Indonesia.

Suharto, by contrast, leaned back the other way, towards Washington. He helped establish ASEAN when it was a narrower organisation, meant to resist the spread of communism in Southeast Asia. But neither leader went all-in with a full alliance either way. And both leaders struggled with the challenges of internal security, keeping this loose collection of thousands of disparate islands, languages, and peoples together.

There was a period of renewed regional engagement after *reformasi*, especially under Hassan Wirajuda, the foreign minister from 2001 to 2009.[228] But, for most of the last decade, the focus has been much more on remaining 'free' than pursuing 'active' policies.[229]

This approach is designed to prevent foreign entanglements from reopening wounds in the Indonesian body politic, whether it be resurgent Islamism, anti-Chinese feeling, or anti-Western sentiment.[230] It is also an implicit acknowledgement of Indonesia's capacity constraints and a reflection of the dominance of the military men and their enduring concerns about internal security. However, with the world around Indonesia changing so fast, 'free and active' is starting to look more like constrained and passive.

Why then do Western governments, from Washington to Canberra, maintain such high expectations for Indonesia to play a bigger, more constructive role in the world? It is partly a function of Indonesia's size, its strategic location in the midst of key global shipping lanes, and its history of, at times, demonstrating leadership potential. It is also partly down to the ability of Jokowi, and his officials, to encourage people to see what they want in him and in Indonesia. Despite the deep historical roots of Indonesia's contemporary aversion to alliances, some Western officials continue mistakenly to believe that Indonesia's warm words signal a desire to become much more engaged in regional and global issues.

The West is desperate for new partners in Asia to help it push back against Xi Jinping's China. Jokowi, however, has no time for great-power politics. He is interested in attracting investment from whomever has the most cash and the fewest conditions. For now, that is the Chinese, who are building roads, bridges, power stations, and ports across Indonesia, in addition to the high-profile Jakarta–Bandung rail link.

Jokowi's concerns about China are not, for the most part, focused on the regional balance of power. His attention is on more narrowly domestic issues, including the bilateral fisheries dispute in the North Natuna Sea, and the potential for tensions with Beijing to undermine him politically or to reignite violence against Indonesia's ethnic Chinese community.

Ultimately, Indonesia's foreign policy is best understood as a reflection of domestic politics, rather than a strategic vision to become a new fulcrum for Asia. The foreign ministry is constrained by Jokowi's obsessive focus on economic diplomacy to support his investment plans.

Jokowi, too, is constrained in his desire to seek friends with benefits by the long-standing domestic opposition to Indonesia becoming too reliant on any single international partner. His unpredictable leadership style is a further constraint on Indonesia's ability to step up on the world stage. In foreign policy, as in other areas, Jokowi and Indonesia appear to be stumbling from one dilemma to the next. It does not amount to a grand strategy. But that is the leader and the nation we see before us.

Why we keep getting Indonesia wrong

Contradictions do not rest easily in the minds of many officials, investors, or analysts. We are engaged in a relentless search for easy, often mono-causal explanations for the fiendishly complex world around us. As a foreign correspondent, I saw the worst of journalism's tendency to 'simplify and exaggerate'. Academics and policy analysts often engage in their own version of this propensity, trying to squeeze and shape a country, politician, or event into a single, overarching theoretical framework. That is one reason why we keep getting Indonesia, and Jokowi, wrong.

The man who has dominated Indonesian politics for nearly a decade, and will continue to lead it for another four years, is a 'bundle of contradictions', in the words of one of his ministers. He capitalised on Indonesia's second experiment with democracy to go from provincial obscurity to the presidency, pitching himself as the outsider who would shake up a broken system. But he proved a poor custodian of democratic principles and practice. Did power change him, or did it just reveal his true character?

It is fiendishly difficult to conjure up an accurate political label for Jokowi. Many hoped he would be a reformer, but that description rings hollow today. He was once an outsider, but, after years of high-level politicking, he is certainly an insider now. Some have called him a populist. But he mostly works with the elite, and he doesn't frame them as the enemy of the people, as populists do.

What we know for sure is that after just six years in the presidential palace, he has lurched back towards Indonesia's authoritarian roots, eroding free speech and the rights of minorities, undermining the all-important fight against corruption, and launching his own nascent political dynasty.

A Muslim who embraced the traditional superstitions of Central Java and did much of his best work alongside two Christian deputies, Jokowi cut one of them adrift to save himself and embraced intolerant religious conservatives to stay in power. Above all, Jokowi's legacy is likely to be weighed by his impact on the economy – his overriding passion. But even there, his enthusiasm and dogged groundwork has been undermined by his incoherent vision and his limited understanding of the complex machinery of government.

We can see the contradictions and paradoxes in his character and life story, as well as his policy record. He came from humble beginnings and he possesses an unrivalled ability to click with voters. But, by the time he ran for mayor of Solo, he was a wealthy emerging patrician. A man who seemed obsessed with small details at times, he has grown impatient with expert advice. Jokowi built his furniture business and his political career on gut instinct. His innate feel for retail politics propelled him to the top at a dizzying speed. However, his impulsiveness cuts against many of his objectives as a national leader.

The president's leadership style continues to confound. Sometimes, he seems to be a puppet of the elites, manipulated by Megawati to give jobs to her fellow travellers. At other times, he pulls the rug from under the feet of Megawati, Prabowo, and the various Jakarta politicians who thought they could control the small businessman from Solo.

However much he disappoints activists and mystifies outsiders, we must remember that Jokowi has consistently been the clear-cut choice of the Indonesian people. He won two resounding victories in the world's biggest direct presidential election – divisive Indonesian politicians cannot hide behind an electoral college as they can in the United States. Jokowi's approval ratings have also remained high, with numbers that would make his foreign counterparts envious.[231]

And yet, the longer Jokowi has spent in the palace, the more he has developed a hard edge to his normally even-handed Javanese ways. The president from the party of Sukarno's family has showed ever more flashes of Suharto-like toughness.

Niccolò Machiavelli famously claimed that 'it is much safer to be feared than loved'.[232] Not the sort of man to seek advice from *The Prince* or any other political treatise, Jokowi has increasingly tried to be both feared and loved. However, his leadership remains brittle. He seems to wither in the face of unexpected crises, from the anti-Ahok movement to COVID-19.

Political scientist Benedict Anderson argued that the Javanese tradition of political thought prioritises the concentration of power, not its use. Long before Jokowi entered politics, Anderson wrote that 'the most obvious sign of the man of Power' is his ability to 'focus his own inner Power, to absorb Power from the outside, and to concentrate within himself apparently antagonistic opposites'.[233] It sounds uncannily like Jokowi.

Once the president had finally defeated his backer-turned-adversary, Prabowo, he absorbed him into his cabinet. But was this a Javanese ploy by Jokowi to boost his own power, or mere realpolitik, ensuring Prabowo could not cause more trouble outside the tent? Although Jokowi sometimes acts like a Javanese king at court, he is living in a very different Indonesia, shaped by a protracted and persistent struggle to build a modern, prosperous nation out of the arbitrary territorial limits of Dutch colonial expansion.

Jokowi's inner contradictions are, in many ways, an embodiment of the contradictions inherent in modern Indonesia's 75 years of history. The country is still struggling to answer foundational questions about the basis of the economy, the political system, and the role of Islam in the state and society.

With a deep-seated aversion to liberal economics, Indonesia will not wholeheartedly embrace free markets and free trade any time soon, despite the preferences of the World Bank and Wall Street. But neither is Jokowi likely to set out a detailed vision for protectionist industrial policy, fearful of the impact on the flows of foreign debt and foreign investment that keep the economy ticking along.

Similarly, Indonesia is caught in a bind between its deep authoritarian foundations and the promise of democracy. Indonesian voters, who have embraced free and fair elections with turnouts that put Western democracies to shame, do not seem ready to accept a Suharto- or Sukarno-style takeover for now. However, many do not share the liberal views of democracy that the Western world too often imagines it sees in Indonesia.[234]

Cynics will say that the authoritarian turn under Jokowi, and the enduring elite control over Indonesian politics and business, makes the country merely a 'procedural democracy'. But getting these electoral procedures right is not easy in a nation transitioning from decades of autocratic rule – Indonesia's troubled neighbours Thailand and Myanmar are examples of just how hard it is. There is still much to fight for in Indonesia's democracy, even if the battle will be unremitting.

Indonesia is not a model of tolerant Islam, but nor is it on the cusp of becoming the next Syria or Iran, let alone the next Malaysia or Brunei. It is not about to throw open its economy and lead a new generation of Asian Tigers. However, it is not going to fully embrace autarky again either, after Sukarno's disastrous experiment with self-reliance. Likewise, the struggle between democracy and authoritarianism will persist for years to come.

By exploring the chronic nature of these frictions, I hope that this book will finally put to rest the idea that 'Indonesia is at a crossroads'.[235] This phrase, which is almost as old as Indonesia itself, has been trotted out so often over the decades that it was once even mocked on *The Simpsons*.[236] The image of a crossroads misleadingly implies that Indonesia faces simple choices about future policies, and takes no account of the enduring weight of its extensive historical baggage.

Jokowi's remarkable rise shows that leaders are not paralysed by their history. They can change its future course. But they are conditioned and constrained by what has gone before. Rather than finding the straightforward Indonesia story we want to see and being endlessly disappointed, we need to embrace the contradictions at the heart of this fascinating and important nation.

This book is not the last word on Jokowi's Indonesia. On the contrary, I hope it prompts others to dig deeper into the people and the forces shaping this nation, climbing out of the silos in which so many researchers get stuck. I also hope that it provokes a fuller debate about Indonesian history and its connection to contemporary politics, economics, and society.

The creation of an Indonesian state was unimaginable to most of the citizens of its disparate provinces and ethnic groups until the moment that it happened.[237] It is incredible that this diverse nation of thousands of islands and hundreds of languages and cultures has survived as a unitary state, through civil wars, coup attempts, genocidal violence, insurgencies, and outside meddling.

Yet, Indonesia remains a nation in the making, and Jokowi's travails are testament to the enormous challenges it faces. If it is to have any chance of meeting the president's grand ambitions to become a developed nation by 2045, Indonesia will need more than technocratic fixes. It must resolve the great unanswered questions of modern Indonesian history.

Former Finance Minister Chatib Basri once told me: 'Indonesia always disappoints. It disappoints the optimists and it disappoints the pessimists too.' It is a somewhat comforting view of an Indonesia that always scrapes through, despite the worst fears about balkanisation, political unrest, and Islamic radicalisation, and despite the highest hopes that it can become an economic powerhouse, a diplomatic fulcrum, and a beacon for democracy.

Jokowi still has four years to go, and it seems he will do little more than muddle through his final term as president. He may once more demonstrate that being underestimated is his greatest strength. I hope so. But I fear that while Jokowi's story shows what is possible in Indonesia, it also shows the limits.

Endnotes

1   Solo is officially called Surakarta, but popularly known
    as Solo.

2   Andrew Thornley, 'Jakarta Elections Test Indonesia's
    Democratic Maturity', *In Asia Insights and Analysis*,
    Asia Foundation, 25 July 2012, https://asiafoundation.
    org/2012/07/25/jakarta-elections-test-indonesias-
    democratic-maturity/.

3   Ben Bland, 'Underdog Set for Jakarta Poll Victory',
    Financial Times, 11 July 2012, https://www.ft.com/
    content/581c6f34-cb4d-11e1-b896-00144feabdc0.

4   The official statistics agency predicts that Indonesia's
    population will reach 271 million in 2020, https://www.
    kompas.com/skola/read/2020/01/08/060000069/jumlah-
    penduduk-indonesia-2020?page=1.com/skola/read/2020/01/
    08/060000069/jumlah-penduduk-indonesia-2020?page=1.

5   Eko Sulistyo, *Jokoway: Jalan Kepemimpinan Jokowi*
    (Jakarta: Moka Media, 2019), 44.

6   Karina M. Tehusijarana, '"The Main Thing is Not the
    Process, but the Result"': Jokowi's full inauguration

speech', *Jakarta Post*, 20 October 2019, https://www.thejakartapost.com/news/2019/10/20/the-main-thing-is-not-the-process-but-the-result-jokowis-full-inauguration-speech.html.

7   Arlina Arshad, 'Joko Widodo, a Deft Hand at Domestic Politics and Global Affairs, is The Straits Times Asian of the Year 2019', *The Straits Times*, 5 December 2019, https://www.straitstimes.com/singapore/jokowi-a-deft-hand-at-domestic-politics-and-global-affairs.

8   Malcolm Turnbull, *A Bigger Picture* (Richmond: Hardie Grant Books, 2020), 292 and 484.

9   Sana Jaffrey, 'Coronavirus Blunders in Indonesia Turn Crisis Into Catastrophe', *Carnegie Endowment for International Peace*, 29 April 2020, https://carnegieendowment.org/2020/04/29/coronavirus-blunders-in-indonesia-turn-crisis-into-catastrophe-pub-81684.

10 'Indonesia Warns on COVID-19 Poverty Setback as Regional Elections Postponed', Reuters, 6 May 2020, https://uk.reuters.com/article/uk-health-coronavirus-indonesia-cases/indonesia-warns-on-covid-19-poverty-setback-as-regional-elections-postponed-idUKKBN22I19T.

11 Interview with author.

12 Interview with author.

13 Alberthiene Endah, *Jokowi: Menuju Cahaya* (Solo: Tiga Serangkai, 2019), 46.

14 Ibid, 27–28.

15 Ibid, 32.

16 Marcus Mietzner, *Reinventing Asian Populism: Jokowi's Rise, Democracy, and Political Contestation In Indonesia* (Honolulu: East–West Center, 2015), 25, https://www.eastwestcenter.org/system/tdf/private/ps072.pdf?file=1&type=node&id=35018.

17 *Konfrontasi* (the Indonesia–Malaysia confrontation) was
    an undeclared 'war' fought between 1963 and 1966
    and stemmed from President Sukarno's opposition
    to the formation of Malaysia. See Adam Leong Kok Wey,
    'The War That Gave Birth to ASEAN', *The Diplomat*,
    9 September 2016, https://thediplomat.com/2016/09/the-
    war-that-gave-birth-to-asean/.

18 For a full account of Suharto's seizure of power and the
    violence that accompanied it, see John Roosa, *Pretext
    for Mass Murder: The September 30th Movement and
    Suharto's Coup d'État in Indonesia* (Madison: University
    of Wisconsin Press, 2006).

19 Alberthiene, *Jokowi: Menuju Cahaya*, 38.

20 Ibid, 51.

21 Amount calculated based on historic exchange rate using
    figures cited in Wawan Mas'udi, 'Creating Legitimacy in
    Decentralized Indonesia: Joko "Jokowi" Widodo's Path to
    Legitimacy In Solo, 2005–2012', PhD thesis (University of
    Melbourne, 2017), 131, https://minerva-access.unimelb.
    edu.au/bitstream/handle/11343/127411/754537Masud
    i_PhDThesis.pdf?sequence=1&isAllowed=y.

22 Ibid, 129.

23 Alberthiene, *Jokowi: Menuju Cahaya*, 62.

24 Ibid, 57–58.

25 Wawan, 'Creating Legitimacy in Decentralized Indonesia',
    163.

26 Alberthiene, *Jokowi: Menuju Cahaya*, 16.

27 Wawan, 'Creating Legitimacy in Decentralized Indonesia',
    140.

28 For an analysis of why decentralisation has often failed
    to lead to improved local governance in Indonesia,

see Thomas B. Pepinsky and Maria M. Wihardja, 'Decentralization and Economic Performance In Indonesia', *Journal of East Asian Studies* 11 (2011), 337–371, https://www.cambridge.org/core/services/aop-cambridge-core/content/view/85542F9E6697311F6F2688 5E75A41B03/S1598240800007372a.pdf/decentralization_and_economic_performance_in_indonesia.pdf.

29   Turnbull, *A Bigger Picture*, 292.

30   Herbert Feith and Lance Castles, *Indonesian Political Thinking 1945–1965* (Ithaca and London: Cornell University Press, 1970), 82.

31   Bland, *Politics in Indonesia: Resilient Elections, Defective Democracy*, Lowy Institute Analysis (Sydney: Lowy Institute for International Policy, 2019), https://www.lowyinstitute.org/publications/politics-indonesia-resilient-elections-defective-democracy.

32   See, for example, Christian von Lübke, 'Maverick Mayor to Presidential Hopeful', *Inside Indonesia*, 23 February 2014, https://www.insideindonesia.org/maverick-mayor-to-presidential-hopeful.

33   See, for example, Richard Javad Heydarian, 'A Revolution Betrayed: The Tragedy of Indonesia's Jokowi', Al Jazeera, 25 November 2019, https://www.aljazeera.com/indepth/opinion/revolution-betrayed-tragedy-indonesia-jokowi-191124104212545.html.

34   Heyder Affan, 'Joko Widodo: "Wali Kota PKL", gaya blusukan, hoaks PKI, dan suara-suara dari Solo', BBC News Indonesia, 17 April 2019, https://www.bbc.com/indonesia/indonesia-47479443.

35   The last two paragraphs draw on the detailed research in Wawan Mas'udi, 'Creating Legitimacy in Decentralized Indonesia', 133–153.

36 Bland, 'The Small-Town Mr Clean Turned "Accidental" President', *Financial Times*, 26 July 2014, https://www. ft.com/content/5391098c1328-11e4-8244-00144feabdc0.

37 Rushda Majeed, *Defusing a Volatile City, Igniting Reforms: Joko Widodo and Surakarta, Indonesia 2005–2011*, Innovations for Successful Societies (Princeton: Princeton University, 2012), 2, https://successfulsocieties.princeton. edu/sites/successfulsocieties/files/Indonesia%20Defusing_ ToU_1.pdf.

38 Bland, 'Joko Widodo—Furniture Maker to Presidential Candidate', *Financial Times*, 25 June 2014, https://youtu. be/3kOm3dQPMvc.

39 Interview with author.

40 For a full examination of how corruption thrived amid democratisation, see Edward Aspinall and Ward Berenschot, *Democracy for Sale: Elections, Clientelism and the State in Indonesia* (Ithaca and London: Cornell University Press, 2019).

41 Transparency International's Corruption Perceptions Index is a well-respected benchmark, https://www.transparency. org/cpi2019.

42 Johannes Nugroho, 'Can Indonesia's Anti-Corruption Agency Survive the Latest Attack by its Powerful Enemies?', *Today*, 12 September 2019, https://www. todayonline.com/commentary/can-indonesias-anti-corruption-agency-survive-latest-attack-its-powerful-enemies.

43 Majeed, *Defusing a Volatile City*.

44 US Embassy telegram, 'Good Governance Antidote to Radicalism in Solo, Central Java', 1 May 2009, (leaked and published by WikiLeaks), https://search.wikileaks.org/ plusd/cables/09JAKARTA773_a.html.

45 'Kemenangan Fenomenal Jokowi-Rudy', *Kompas*, 21 May 2010, https://regional.kompas.com/read/2010/05/21/ 03402631/Kemenangan.Fenomenal.Jokowi-Rudy? page=all.

46 Bland, 'Jakarta Faces Close-Shave Election Fight', *Financial Times*, 10 July 2012, https://www.ft.com/ content/92005d3c-c986-11e1-97cd-00144feabdc0.

47 Bland, 'Jokowi Stops Traffic in Fight for Jakarta', *Financial Times*, 17 September 2012, https://www.ft.com/content/ f8f84172-fd74-11e1-8e36-00144feabdco.

48 Bland, 'Outsider Set for Victory in Jakarta Poll', *Financial Times*, 20 September 2012, https://www.ft.com/ content/674b3f1e-030e-11e2-a284-00144feabdc0.

49 'Mampukah Jokowi menertibkan warga Jakarta?', *Kontan*, 2 December 2013, https://nasional.kontan.co.id/news/ mampukah-jokowi-menertibkan-warga-jakarta.

50 Mietzner, 'Reinventing Asian Populism', 45.

51 Bland, 'Politics in Indonesia'.

52 Bland, 'The Small-Town Mr Clean Turned "Accidental" President'.

53 Alberthiene, *Jokowi: Menuju Cahaya*, 65.

54 Ibid, 361–62.

55 Transcript of BBC interview with Jokowi, 13 February 2020, https://www.bbc.com/indonesia/indonesia-51382305.

56 For more on the power and limits of local political dynasties in Indonesia, see Michael Buehler, 'The Ephemeral Nature of Local Political Monopolies', in Robert W. Hefner, *Routledge Handbook of Contemporary Indonesia* (Abingdon: Routledge, 2018), https:// michaelbuehler.asia/wp-content/uploads/2018/01/ BuehlerMonopolies2018.pdf.

57　'John Emerich Edward Dalberg, Lord Acton', Online Library of Liberty, https://oll.libertyfund.org/titles/acton-acton-creighton-correspondence#Acton_PowerCorrupts1524_24.

58　Chris McGreal, 'Robert Caro: A Life with LBJ and the Pursuit of Power', *The Guardian*, 10 June 2012, https://www.theguardian.com/world/2012/jun/10/lyndon-b-johnson-robert-caro-biography.

59　In November 2013, for example, one poll showed that only 6 per cent of Indonesians wanted to see Megawati become their next president, compared to 37 per cent for Jokowi, http://www.roymorgan.com/findings/5319-indonesian-vote-october-2013-201311252157.

60　Lionel Barber, David Pilling and Ben Bland, 'Bakrie Sets Sights on Indonesia's Top Job', *Financial Times*, 3 April 2013, https://www.ft.com/content/eadd10ea-9784-11e2-b7ef-00144feabdc0.

61　Mietzner, 'Reinventing Asian Populism', 30–31.

62　Ibid, 42.

63　Aaron Connelly, 'Indonesian Election: Prabowo Now the Favourite', *The Interpreter*, 24 June 2014, https://www.lowyinstitute.org/the-interpreter/indonesian-election-prabowo-now-favourite.

64　Helen Pausacker, 'Born to Rule; Trained to Fight; Determined to Win', *Indonesia at Melbourne*, 3 June 2014, https://indonesiaatmelbourne.unimelb.edu.au/born-to-rule-trained-to-fight-determined-to-win/.

65　For a good example of Prabowo's fiery rhetoric, see 'Gaya Berapi-Api Orasi Prabowo di Medan', *Detik News*, 11 June 2014, https://news.detik.com/berita/2605434/gaya-berapi-api-orasi-prabowo-di-medan?991101mainnews=.

66　Edward Aspinall and Marcus Mietzner, 'Indonesian Politics in 2014: Democracy's Close Call', *Bulletin of Indonesian*

Economic Studies 50, No 3 (2014), https://openresearch-repository.anu.edu.au/bitstream/1885/15088/2/01%20Aspinall%20%20and%20Mietzner%20Indonesian%20politics%20in%202014.pdf; and Vannessa Hearman, 'Spectre of Anti-Communist Smears Resurrected Against Jokowi', *The Conversation*, 4 July 2014, https://theconversation.com/spectre-of-anti-communist-smears-resurrected-against-jokowi-28730.

67 Bland, 'Jokowi Confident of Victory Despite Squandering Poll Lead', *Financial Times*, 30 June 2014, https://www.ft.com/content/e407a484-0028-11e4-8aaf-00144feab7de.

68 Eric C. Thompson, *Indonesia in Transition: The 1999 Presidential Elections*, National Bureau of Asian Research, Policy Report No 9, December 1999, http://profile.nus.edu.sg/fass/socect/Thompson%201999%20NBR%20Briefing.pdf.

69 Dan Slater, 'Party Cartelization, Indonesian-Style: Presidential Power-Sharing and the Contingency of Democratic Opposition', *Journal of East Asian Studies* 18, No 1 (2018), 2346.

70 Edward Aspinall, Diego Fossati, Burhanuddin Muhtadi and Eve Warburton, 'Mapping the Indonesian Political Spectrum', *New Mandala*, 24 April 2018, https://www.newmandala.org/mapping-indonesian-political-spectrum/.

71 For a more detailed analysis of this trend, see Michael Buehler and Dani Muhtada, 'Democratization and The Diffusion of Shari'a Law: Comparative Insights from Indonesia', *South East Asia Research* 24, No 2 (2016), https://journals.sagepub.com/doi/abs/10.1177/0967828X16649311.

72 Devina Halim, 'PKS Berjanji Hapus Pajak Sepeda Motor dan Berlakukan SIM Seumur Hidup', *Kompas*, 22 November 2018, https://nasional.kompas.com/read/2018/11/22/14484091/pks-berjanji-hapus-pajak-sepeda-motor-dan-berlakukan-sim-seumur-hidup.

73 Ulla Fionna, 'Indonesian Parties Twenty Years On: Personalism and Professionalism Amidst Dealignment,' 23 in Max Lane, *Continuity and Change After Indonesia's Reforms: Contributions to an Ongoing Assessment* (Singapore: ISEAS Publishing, 2019).

74 'Joko Widodo Wins Indonesia Presidential Election', BBC News, 22 July 2014, https://www.bbc.com/news/world-asia-28415536.

75 'Jokowi's Volunteers to Continue Movement', *Jakarta Post*, 23 October 2014, https://www.thejakartapost.com/news/2014/10/23/jokowi-s-volunteers-continue-movement.html.

76 Abdil Mughis Mudhoffir, 'Indonesia's New Cabinet Built on Political Transactions', *The Conversation*, 1 August 2016, https://theconversation.com/indonesias-new-cabinet-built-on-political-transactions-63196.

77 Interview with author.

78 Max Lane, 'Indonesia's New Politics: Transaction Without Contestation', in Lane, *Continuity and Change After Indonesia's Reforms*, 16.

79 David Halberstam, 'The Vantage Point: Perspectives of the Presidency 1963–1969. By Lyndon Baines Johnson', *The New York Times*, 31 October 1971, https://www.nytimes.com/1971/10/31/archives/the-vantage-point-perspectives-of-the-presidency-19631969-by-lyndon.html.

80 Koichi Kawamura, *Consensus and Democracy in Indonesia: Musyawarah-Mufakat Revisited*, Institute of Developing Economies Discussion Paper 308 (Chiba, Japan: IDE JETRO, September 2011), file:///C:/Temporary%20Documents/Lee/Consensus_and_Democracy_in_Indonesia_Musyawarah-Mu.pdf.

81 'Indonesian Minister Sparks Anger with HIV Comments', Agence France-Presse, 5 February 2015, https://news. yahoo.com/indonesian-minister-sparks-anger-hiv-comments-204239967.html.

82 Marchio Irfan Gorbiano and Rizki Fachriansyah, '"It's Our Nation's Right to Rely on the Almighty": Minister Justifies Calling for Prayers in Coronavirus Battle', *Jakarta Post*, 17 February 2020, https://www.thejakartapost. com/news/2020/02/17/its-our-nations-right-to-rely-on-the-almighty-minister-justifies-calling-for-prayers-in-coronavirus-battle.html.

83 See Richard C. Paddock, 'Indonesian General Accused of Kidnapping is Named Defense Minister', *The New York Times*, 23 October 2019, https://www.nytimes.com/2019/10/23/world/asia/indonesia-prabowo-joko-widodo.html; and 'Indonesia: Indicted General Unfit for Cabinet Post', *Human Rights Watch*, 28 July 2016, https://www.hrw.org/news/2016/07/28/indonesia-indicted-general-unfit-cabinet-post.

84 Burhanuddin Muhtadi, 'Jokowi's First Year: A Weak President Caught between Reform and Oligarchic Politics', *Bulletin of Indonesian Economic Studies* 51, No 3 (2015), 349–368.

85 Interview with author.

86 Interview with author.

87 Roland Rajah, *Indonesia's Economy: Between Growth and Stability*, Lowy Institute Analysis, (Sydney: Lowy Institute for International Policy, 2018), https://www.lowyinstitute. org/publications/indonesia-economy-between-growth-and-stability.

88 Interview with author.

89 A good example of this was the prosecution and jailing of several mid-level employees of Chevron, the US oil company, on questionable corruption charges: 'Indonesian Graft Court Jails Third Chevron Employee', Agence France-

Presse, 20 July 2013, https://sg.news.yahoo.com/indonesian-graft-court-jails-third-chevron-employee-170502811.html.

90   Yenny Tjoe, 'Two Decades of Economic Growth Benefited Only the Richest 20%. How Severe is Inequality in Indonesia?', *The Conversation*, 28 August 2018, https://theconversation.com/two-decades-of-economic-growth-benefited-only-the-richest-20-how-severe-is-inequality-in-indonesia-101138.

91   'Percentage of Poor People 2007–2019', Badan Pusat Statistik, https://www.bps.go.id/dynamictable/2016/08/18/1219/persentase-penduduk-miskin-menurut-provinsi-2007---2019.html.

92   'Indonesia Warns on COVID-19 Poverty Setback as Regional Elections Postponed', Reuters, 6 May 2020, https://www.reuters.com/article/us-health-coronavirus-indonesia-election/indonesia-warns-on-covid-19-poverty-setback-as-regional-elections-postponed-idUSKBN22I1M9.

93   World Bank, 'Aspiring Indonesia: Expanding the Middle Class', 30 January 2020, https://www.worldbank.org/en/country/indonesia/publication/aspiring-indonesia-expanding-the-middle-class.

94   Arys Aditya, Tassia Sipahutar, and Rieka Rahadiana, 'Indonesia's President Vows Tougher Economic Reforms After Clearing Elections', Bloomberg News, 9 May 2019, https://www.bloomberg.com/news/articles/2019-05-09/with-elections-no-longer-a-worry-jokowi-vows-tougher-reforms.

95   Ben Bland and Avantika Chilkoti, 'Widodo Shuns Grand Plan for Nuts and Bolts Approach', *Financial Times*, 16 April 2016, https://www.ft.com/content/b8a0ea4a-0165-11e6-99cb-83242733f755.

96   For a deeper analysis of Jokowi and developmentalism, see Eve Warburton, 'Jokowi and the New Developmentalism', *Bulletin of Indonesian Economic Studies* 52, No 3 (2016), 297–320.

97 Interview with author.

98 'Jejaring Kuasa Sang Jenderal', *Tempo*, 25 April 2016, https://majalah.tempo.co/read/laporan-utama/150572/jejaring-kuasa-sang-jenderal?.

99 'Jokowi Gives Minister Luhut More Powers Through New Regulation', *Jakarta Post*, 6 November 2019, https://www.thejakartapost.com/news/2019/11/05/jokowi-gives-minister-luhut-more-powers-through-new-regulation.html.

100 Kornelius Purba, 'Gen. Luhut: Jokowi's Much Hated and Loved COVID-19 Frontman', *Jakarta Post*, 21 April 2020, https://www.thejakartapost.com/academia/2020/04/21/gen-luhut-jokowis-much-hated-and-loved-covid-19-frontman.html.

101 Alberthiene, *Jokowi Menuju Cahaya*, 83.

102 For an insightful account of how issues of poor infrastructure and inefficient bureaucracy damage fishermen's incomes in this part of Indonesia, and the advantages of better connectivity with the Philippines, see Elizabeth Pisani, *Indonesia Etc: Exploring the Improbable Nation* (London: Granta, 2014), 211–212.

103 Antonio L. Colina IV, 'Presidents Duterte and Widodo Launch Davao–GenSan–Bitung Shipping Route', *Minda News*, April 30 2017, https://www.mindanews.com/business/2017/04/presidents-duterte-and-widodo-launch-davao-gensan-bitung-shipping-route/.

104 'Presiden Teken Inpres "Refocussing" Kegiatan, Realokasi Anggaran, serta Pengadaan Barang dan Jasa', Sekretariat Kabinet Republik Indonesia, 23 March 2020, https://setkab.go.id/presiden-teken-inpres-refocussing-kegiatan-realokasi-anggaran-serta-pengadaan-barang-dan-jasa/.

105 Data from World Bank, https://data.worldbank.org/indicator/GC.TAX.TOTL.GD.ZS.

106 For the latest rankings, see https://www.doingbusiness.org/
en/rankings.

107 'Menkominfo: Ego Sektoral adalah Musuh Bersama',
Republika, 25 August 2015, https://nasional.republika.
co.id/berita/nasional/umum/15/08/25/ntn5qc284-
menkominfo-ego-sektoral-adalah-musuh-bersama.

108 Ameidyo Daud, 'Jokowi Tegur Para Pejabat Karena
Sweeping Tenaga Kerja Asing', Katadata, 6 March 2018,
https://katadata.co.id/berita/2018/03/06/jokowi-tegur-para-
pejabat-karena-sweeping-tenaga-kerja-asing.

109 Interviews with author.

110 'Indonesia e-Commerce Execs Say New Rules May
Choke Booming Online Growth', Reuters, 10 December
2019, https://www.reuters.com/article/indonesia-
ecommerce/indonesia-e-commerce-execs-say-new-rules-
may-choke-booming-online-growth-idUSL4N28K1J1.

111 Rachmadea Aisyah, 'Indonesia's Latest Economic Stimulus
Package: What You Need to Know', *Jakarta Post*,
19 November 2018, https://www.thejakartapost.com/
news/2018/11/17/indonesias-latest-economic-stimulus-
package-what-you-need-to-know.html.

112 Arianto Patunru and Sjamsu Rahardja, *Trade Protectionism
in Indonesia: Bad Times and Bad Policy*, Lowy Institute
Analysis (Sydney: Lowy Institute for International Policy,
2015), https://www.lowyinstitute.org/publications/trade-
protectionism-indonesia-bad-times-and-bad-policy.

113 'Government Not Involved in Esemka Car Production:
Jokowi', *Jakarta Post*, 26 October 2018, https://www.
thejakartapost.com/news/2018/10/26/government-not-
involved-in-esemka-car-production-jokowi.html.
A previous attempt by Tommy Suharto, the autocratic
ruler's son, to launch a national car had predictably ended
in financial collapse and allegations of corruption.

See 'Suharto Son Sues Indonesian Minister Over Car Case', Reuters, 12 August 2008, https://www.reuters.com/article/us-indonesia-suharto/suharto-son-sues-indonesian-minister-over-car-case-idUSJAK12759120080812.

114 Bland, 'Hopes Rise that Widodo Will Inject New Life into Indonesia Reform', *Financial Times*, 19 October 2014, https://www.ft.com/content/51690c00-47b6-11e4-be7b-00144feab7de.

115 'OECD Economic Surveys: Indonesia', October 2018, 26, http://www.oecd.org/economy/surveys/Indonesia-2018-OECD-economic-survey-overview.pdf.

116 Jeffrey Hutton, 'Indonesia's State-Owned Firms Face Big Overhaul', *The Straits Times*, 11 March 2020, https://www.straitstimes.com/asia/se-asia/indonesias-state-owned-firms-face-big-overhaul.

117 Feith and Castles, *Indonesian Political Thinking*, 392–395.

118 Republic of Indonesia, Indonesian Constitution, http://www.dpr.go.id/jdih/uu1945.

119 Hal Hill and Deasy Pane, 'Indonesia and the Global Economy: Missed Opportunities?' 272 in Arianto A. Patunru, Mari Pangestu and M. Chatib Basri, *Indonesia in the New World: Globalisation, Nationalism and Sovereignty* (Singapore: ISEAS Publishing, 2018).

120 Feith and Castles, *Indonesian Political Thinking*, 379–381.

121 Sadli's Law is named after a leading technocrat who was an influential minister during the Suharto years. See Hal Hill and Deasy Pane, 'Indonesia and the Global Economy: Missed Opportunities?', 272.

122 Interview with author.

123 Ibid.

124 Tim Lindsey and Tim Mann, 'Indonesia was in Denial Over Coronavirus. Now it May Be Facing a Looming Disaster', *The Conversation*, 8 April 2020, https://theconversation. com/indonesia-was-in-denial-over-coronavirus-now-it-may-be-facing-a-looming-disaster-135436.

125 Ardila Syakriah, 'COVID-19: Anies Slams Health Ministry's Requirements for Large-Scale Social Restrictions', *Jakarta Post*, 5 April 2020, https://www.thejakartapost.com/ news/2020/04/05/covid-19-anies-slams-health-ministrys-requirements-for-large-scale-social-restrictions.html.

126 Tangguh Chairil, 'Indonesia Needs to Change its Security-Heavy Approach to COVID-19', *The Diplomat*, 30 April 2020, https://thediplomat.com/2020/04/indonesia-needs-to-change-its-security-heavy-approach-to-covid-19/.

127 Dyna Rochmyaningsih, 'Indonesian Scientists Say Government Snubs Offers to Help Fight Coronavirus', *Science*, 18 April 2020, https://www.sciencemag.org/ news/2020/04/open-doors-us-indonesian-scientists-say-government-snubs-offers-help-fight-coronavirus.

128 Hellena Souisa, 'Kunci Penanganan Virus Corona di Indonesia ada pada Keterbukaan dan Ketegasan Pemerintah', ABC News Indonesian Service, 31 March 2020, https://www. abc.net.au/indonesian/2020-03-31/melihat-penanganan-virus-corona-selama-sebulan/12102618.

129 'Indonesian Capital Still Sinking, Despite Groundwater Improvements', Reuters, 15 October 2019, https://www. reuters.com/article/us-indonesia-capital/indonesian-capital-still-sinking-despite-groundwater-improvements-idUSKBN1WU1JI.

130 Jokowi's State Address to the Parliament, 19 August 2019, https://setkab.go.id/en/state-address-of-the-president-of-the-republic-of-indonesia-on-the-occasion-of-the-74th-anniversary-of-the-proclamation-of-independence-of-the-republic-of-indonesia-before-the-joint-session-of-the-r/.

131 Interview with author.

132 Benedict Anderson, *Language and Power: Exploring Political Cultures in Indonesia* (Ithaca: Cornell University Press, 1990), 41.

133 Alberthiene, *Jokowi Menuju Cahaya*, 153–154.

134 'BPS: 59% of Indonesia Economy Concentrated in Java', *Tempo*, 5 February 2020, https://en.tempo.co/read/1303990/bps-59-of-indonesia-economy-concentrated-in-java.

135 'Muhammad Jusuf Kalla, Vice President: President Needs Ministers Who Can Do Their Job Well', *Tempo*, 10 September 2019, https://magz.tempo.co/read/35903/muhammad-jusuf-kalla-vice-president-president-needs-ministers-who-can-do-their-job-well.

136 Interview with author.

137 See, for example, then President Barack Obama's speech at the University of Indonesia on 10 November 2010, entitled 'Indonesia's Example To the World', https://obamawhitehouse.archives.gov/blog/2010/11/10/president-obama-jakarta-indonesia-s-example-world.

138 Simon Butt, 'Why is Ahok in Prison? A Legal Analysis of the Decision', *Indonesia at Melbourne*, 6 June 2017, https://indonesiaatmelbourne.unimelb.edu.au/why-is-ahok-in-prison-a-legal-analysis-of-the-decision/.

139 Greg Fealy, 'Race, Faith and Ahok's Defeat', *The Strategist*, 21 April 2017, https://www.aspistrategist.org.au/race-faith-ahoks-defeat/.

140 'Indonesia Protest: Jakarta Anti-Governor Rally Turns Violent', BBC News, 4 November 2016, https://www.bbc.com/news/world-asia-37856476.

141 Greg Fealy, 'Bigger than Ahok: Explaining the 2 December Mass Rally', *Indonesia at Melbourne*, 7 December 2016,

https://indonesiaatmelbourne.unimelb.edu.au/bigger-than-ahok-explaining-jakartas-2-december-mass-rally/.

142 Alberthiene, *Jokowi Menuju Cahaya*, 295.

143 Interviews by author with advisers to Jokowi and members of his cabinet.

144 'Sambutan Presiden Jokowi di Depan Jutaan Peserta Aksi Damai 212', tvOneNews, 2 December 2016, https://youtu.be/zKily73IPbY.

145 A. S. Hikam, 'Has Jokowi Handed a Strategic Victory to Radicals?', *New Mandala*, 5 December 2016, https://www.newmandala.org/jokowi-hands-strategic-victory-radicals/.

146 Thomas P. Power, 'Jokowi's Authoritarian Turn and Indonesia's Democratic Decline', *Bulletin of Indonesian Economic Studies* 54, No 3 (2018), 307–338, https://www.tandfonline.com/doi/abs/10.1080/00074918.2018.1549918?journalCode=cbic20.

147 Norshahril Saat and Aninda Dewayanti, 'Jokowi's Management of Nahdlatul Ulama (NU): A New Order Approach?', *ISEAS Perspective Issue 2020 No 1*, 3 January 2020, https://www.iseas.edu.sg/wp-content/uploads/pdfs/ISEAS_Perspective_2020_1.pdf.

148 Greg Fealy, 'Jokowi's Bungled Ban of Hizbut Tahrir', *The Interpreter*, 17 July 2017, https://www.lowyinstitute.org/the-interpreter/jokowi-s-bungled-ban-hizbut-tahrir. In May 2017, Habib Rizieq was charged with breaching Indonesia's wide-ranging anti-pornography law, by which point he was in Saudi Arabia from where he is yet to return, 'Rizieq Shihab Named Suspect in Pornography Case While Abroad', *Jakarta Post*, 29 May 2017, https://www.thejakartapost.com/news/2017/05/29/rizieq-shihab-named-suspect-in-pornography-case-while-abroad.html.

149 Evan Laksmana, 'Is Indonesia's Military Eyeing the Republic?', *The New York Times*, 11 April 2019, https://www.nytimes.com/2019/04/11/opinion/joko-widodo-indonesia-military.html.

150 Institute for Policy Analysis of Conflict, *Update on the Indonesian Military's Influence*, IPAC Report No 26, 11 March 2016, 2, http://file.understandingconflict.org/file/2016/03/IPAC_Report_No._26_.pdf.

151 Leonard C. Sebastian, Emirza Adi Syailendra and Keoni Indrabayu Marzuki, 'Civil-Military Relations in Indonesia after the Reform Period', *Asia Policy* 13, No 3 (2018), 49–78.

152 Simon Butt, 'Amendments Spell Disaster for the KPK', *Indonesia at Melbourne*, 18 September 2019, https://indonesiaatmelbourne.unimelb.edu.au/amendments-spell-disaster-for-the-kpk/.

153 'Indonesia President Says No Plan to Drop Controversial Anti-Graft Bill', Reuters, 1 November 2019, https://www.reuters.com/article/us-indonesia-corruption/indonesia-president-says-no-plan-to-drop-controversial-anti-graft-bill-idUSKBN1XB43K.

154 Max Walden, 'Students Dead, Activists Arrested Amid Protests to Stop Legal Changes in Indonesia', ABC News, 2 October 2019, https://www.abc.net.au/news/2019-10-02/students-dead-activists-arrested-amid-protests-in-indonesia/11561714.

155 'Farewell Anti-Corruption Commission', *Tempo*, 3 April 2020, https://en.tempo.co/read/1327289/farewell-anti-corruption-commission.

156 Interview with author.

157 'Tycoon Hary Tanoesoedibjo's Daughter Appointed Deputy Minister', BeritaSatu, 25 October 2019, https://jakartaglobe.id/news/tycoon-hary-tanoesoedibjos-daughter-appointed-deputy-minister/.

158 Interview with author.

159 Bland, 'Lunch with the FT: Prabowo Subianto',
   Financial Times, 28 June 2013, https://www.ft.com/
   content/7024de00-de5b-11e2-b990-00144feab7de.

160 CIA Intelligence Assessment, 'Indonesia: The Cloudy
   Presidential Succession', 30 August 1985, https://
   www.cia.gov/library/readingroom/docs/CIA-
   RDP86T00590R000300450001-3.pdf.

161 Maikel Jefriando and Wilda Asmarini, 'Indonesian
   Protesters Disperse After Second Night of Post-Election
   Unrest', Reuters, 23 May 2019, https://www.reuters.com/
   article/us-indonesia-election/indonesian-protesters-disperse-
   after-second-night-of-post-election-unrest-idUSKCN1ST003.

162 '"I Congratulate Jokowi as President": Prabowo Meets
   Jokowi at MRT Station', *Jakarta Post*, 13 July 2019,
   https://www.thejakartapost.com/news/2019/07/13/i-
   congratulate-jokowi-as-president-prabowo-meets-jokowi-
   at-mrt-station.html.

163 Bland, 'Lunch with the FT: Prabowo Subianto'.

164 Andreas Harsono, 'Indonesia's Religious Minorities Under
   Threat', *Human Rights Watch*, 2 February 2017, https://
   www.hrw.org/news/2017/02/02/indonesias-religious-
   minorities-under-threat.

165 Feith and Castles, *Indonesian Political Thinking*, 193.

166 Edward Aspinall, 'Indonesia's Election and the Return of
   Ideological Competition', *New Mandala*, 22 April 2019,
   https://www.newmandala.org/indonesias-election-and-the-
   return-of-ideological-competition/.

167 'NU, Non-Muslim Voters Held "Key Role" in Jokowi's
   Win', *Jakarta Post*, 25 July 2019, https://www.
   thejakartapost.com/news/2019/07/25/nu-non-muslim-
   voters-held-key-role-jokowi-s-win.html.

168 Bland, 'Indonesian Strongman Lost, but Identity Politics Won', *Australian Financial Review*, 3 May 2019, https://www.afr.com/world/asia/indonesian-strongman-lost-but-identity-politics-won-20190503-p51jtq.

169 Interview with author.

170 Edward Aspinall, Diego Fossati, Burhanuddin Muhtadi and Eve Warburton, 'Elites, Masses, and Democratic Decline in Indonesia' *Democratization* 27, No 4 (2020), 505–526, https://www.tandfonline.com/doi/full/10.1080/13510347.2019.1680971.

171 Ihsanuddin, 'Jokowi: Demokrasi Kita Sudah Kebablasan', *Kompas,* 22 February 2017, https://nasional.kompas.com/read/2017/02/22/12031291/jokowi.demokrasi.kita.sudah.kebablasan.

172 Claudia Stoicescu, 'Why Jokowi's War on Drugs is Doing More Harm Than Good', Al Jazeera, 26 July 2017, https://www.aljazeera.com/indepth/opinion/2017/07/jokowi-war-drugs-harm-good-170725101917170.html.

173 For a more in-depth analysis of Jokowi's Papua policy, see Richard Chauvel, 'Papua Under the Joko Widodo Presidency', 213–237 in Lane, *Continuity and Change After Indonesia's Reforms.*

174 Sam Wanda, 'Indonesia Arrests 34, Blocks Internet in Papua to Curb Protests', Reuters, 22 August 2019, https://www.reuters.com/article/us-indonesia-papua/indonesia-arrests-34-blocks-internet-in-papua-to-curb-protests-idUSKCN1VC0EQ.

175 Benjamin Strick and Famega Syavira, 'Papua Unrest: Social Media Bots "Skewing the Narrative"', BBC News, 11 October 2019, https://www.bbc.com/news/world-asia-49983667.

176 Fanny Potkin, 'Backstory: Hunting for Fake News and Trolls in Indonesia's Elections', Reuters, 29 April 2019,

https://www.reuters.com/article/us-indonesia-election-backstory/backstory-hunting-for-fake-news-and-trolls-in-indonesias-elections-idUSKCN1S50KA.

177 Ross Tapsell, 'Indonesia's Policing of Hoax News Increasingly Politicised', *ISEAS Perspectives Issue 2019*, No 75 (20 September 2019), https://www.iseas.edu.sg/images/pdf/ISEAS_Perspective_2019_75.pdf.

178 'Darurat Corona, Polri Patroli Khusus Pantau Hoax dan Penghinaan Presiden', Detik News, 5 April 2020, https://news.detik.com/berita/d-4966256/darurat-corona-polri-patroli-khusus-pantau-hoax-dan-penghinaan-presiden?utm_source=twitter&utm_campaign=detikcomsocmed&utm_medium=btn&utm_content=news.

179 'Indonesia: Little Transparency in COVID-19 Outbreak', *Human Rights Watch*, https://www.hrw.org/news/2020/04/09/indonesia-little-transparency-covid-19-outbreak.

180 Institute for Policy Analysis of Conflict, *Update on the Indonesian Military's Influence*, IPAC Report No 26, 11 March 2016, 10, http://file.understandingconflict.org/file/2016/03/IPAC_Report_No._26_.pdf.

181 'Temui Moeldoko, Dubes China Jelaskan Soal Uighur Di Xinjiang', Kantor Staf Presiden, 17 December 2019, http://ksp.go.id/temui-moeldoko-dubes-china-jelaskan-soal-uighur-di-xinjiang/index.html.

182 'Menkominfo Akan Usul Revisi UU Penyiaran Masuk Prolegnas 2020', CNN Indonesia, 2 November 2019, https://www.cnnindonesia.com/teknologi/20191101114820-185-444791/menkominfo-akan-usul-revisi-uu-penyiaran-masuk-prolegnas-2020.

183 Tim Lindsey, 'Jokowi in Indonesia's "Neo-New Order"', *East Asia Forum*, 7 November 2017, https://www.eastasiaforum.org/2017/11/07/jokowi-in-indonesias-neo-new-order/.

184 Interview with author.

185 This section draws on R. E. Elson, *Suharto: A Political Biography* (Cambridge: Cambridge University Press, 2001).

186 Karina M. Tehusijarana, 'Lamun sira sekti, aja mateni: Jokowi Infuses Javanese Philosophy into Politics', *Jakarta Post*, 24 July 2019, https://www.thejakartapost.com/news/2019/07/24/lamun-sira-sekti-aja-mateni-jokowi-infuses-javanese-philosophy-into-politics.html.

187 Elson, *Suharto: A Political Biography*, 298.

188 Michael Vatikiotis, *Indonesian Politics Under Suharto: The Rise and Fall of The New Order* (London and New York: Routledge, 1999), 5.

189 Marlinda Oktavia Erwanti, 'Jokowi: Di Indonesia Tak Ada Oposisi, Demokrasi Kita Gotong Royong', Detik.com, 23 October 2019, https://news.detik.com/berita/d-4758805/jokowi-di-indonesia-tak-ada-oposisi-demokrasi-kita-gotong-royong.

190 Feith and Castles, *Indonesian Political Thinking*, 35–37.

191 Sana Jaffrey, 'Is Indonesia Becoming a Two-Tier Democracy?', *Carnegie Endowment for International Peace*, 23 January 2020, https://carnegieendowment.org/2020/01/23/is-indonesia-becoming-two-tier-democracy-pub-80876.

192 'Saving Our Election', *Tempo*, 30 November 2019, https://en.tempo.co/read/1278512/saving-our-election.

193 'Our Democracy at Stake,' *Jakarta Post*, 7 October 2019, https://www.thejakartapost.com/academia/2019/10/07/our-democracy-at-stake.html.

194 Eisya Eloksari, 'Omnibus Bill to Diminish Local Governments' Authority Over Spatial Planning: KPPOD', *Jakarta Post*, 27 February 2020, https://www.thejakartapost.com/news/2020/02/27/omnibus-bill-to-diminish-local-governments-authority-over-spatial-planning-kppod.html.

195 Marchio Irfan Gorbiano and Ghina Ghaliya, 'Turf War Undermines COVID-19 Fight in Indonesia', *Jakarta Post*, 1 April 2020, https://www.thejakartapost.com/news/2020/04/01/turf-war-undermines-covid-19-fight-indonesia-government-jokowi-anies.html.

196 Rendi Witular, 'Presenting Maritime Doctrine', *Jakarta Post*, 14 November 2014, https://www.thejakartapost.com/news/2014/11/14/presenting-maritime-doctrine.html.

197 For example, the US Department of Defence's eagerly awaited Indo–Pacific Strategy Report of 2019 states that 'the United States supports Indonesia's vision to become a "global maritime fulcrum" straddling the Indian and Pacific Oceans', https://media.defense.gov/2019/Jul/01/2002152311/-1/-1/1/DEPARTMENT-OF-DEFENSE-INDO-PACIFIC-STRATEGY-REPORT-2019.PDF.

198 Evan Laksmana, 'Indonesia as Global Maritime Fulcrum: A Post-Mortem Analysis', *Asia Maritime Transparency Initiative*, 8 November 2019, https://amti.csis.org/indonesia-as-global-maritime-fulcrum-a-post-mortem-analysis/.

199 Rendi A. Witular, 'Foreign Friendships Must Benefit RI: Jokowi', *Jakarta Post*, 17 November 2014, https://www.thejakartapost.com/news/2014/11/17/foreign-friendships-must-benefit-ri-jokowi.html.

200 Ted Piccone and Bimo Yusman, 'Indonesian Foreign Policy: "A Million Friends and Zero Enemies"', *Brookings*, 14 February 2014, https://www.brookings.edu/articles/indonesian-foreign-policy-a-million-friends-and-zero-enemies/.

201 For a deeper examination of the ups and downs of SBY's decade in power, see John McBeth, *The Loner: President Yudhoyono's Decade of Trial and Indecision* (Singapore: Straits Times Press, 2016).

202 Alberthiene, *Jokowi Menuju Cahaya*, 302.

203 Linda Yulisman, 'Winter is Coming: Indonesia's President Jokowi Urges Unity as He Sounds Warning for Global Economy', *The Straits Times*, 12 October 2018, https://www.straitstimes.com/asia/se-asia/winter-is-coming-indonesias-president-jokowi-sounds-warning-for-global-economy.

204 Max Walden, 'Indonesian President Arrives in Canberra Bearing "Gift", but Relationship Still Has Long Way to Go', ABC News, 9 February 2020, https://www.abc.net.au/news/2020-02-09/indonesia-australia-trade-deal-relationship-analysis/11946174.

205 Intan Umbari Prihatin, 'Presiden Jokowi: Jika Berdikari Ekonomi, Indonesia Tak Mudah Ditekan Siapapun', Merdeka.com, 10 January 2020, https://www.merdeka.com/peristiwa/presiden-jokowi-jika-berdikari-ekonomi-indonesia-tak-mudah-ditekan-siapapun.html.

206 Anthony Reid, 'Challenging Geography: Asserting Economic Sovereignty in a Porous Archipelago', in Arianto et al, *Indonesia in the New World*, 17–34.

207 James Massola and Amilia Rosa, 'New Indonesian Attorney-General Flags Resumption of Death Penalty', *The Sydney Morning Herald*, 28 October 2019, https://www.smh.com.au/world/asia/new-indonesian-attorney-general-flags-resumption-of-death-penalty-20191028-p534rf.html.

208 Aaron Connelly, 'Sovereignty and the Sea: President Joko Widodo's Foreign Policy Challenges', *Contemporary Southeast Asia* 37, No 1 (2015), 1–28, https://www.lowyinstitute.org/sites/default/files/connelly_-_jokowi_foreign_policy_-_csea_april_2015_0.pdf.

209 Linda Yulisman, 'Jokowi Visits Natuna Islands as Stand-Off with China Continues', *The Straits Times*, 9 January

2020, https://www.straitstimes.com/asia/se-asia/jokowi-visits-natuna-islands-as-stand-off-with-china-continues.

210 Aaron Connelly, 'Indonesia's New North Natuna Sea: What's in a Name?', *The Interpreter*, 19 July 2017, https://www.lowyinstitute.org/the-interpreter/indonesia-s-new-north-natuna-sea-what-s-name.

211 Evan Laksmana, 'Why Indonesia's Natuna Base is Not About Deterring China', *Asia Maritime Transparency Initiative*, 25 January 2019, https://amti.csis.org/indonesias-natuna-base-not-about-deterring-china/.

212 Laksmana, 'Indonesia as Global Maritime Fulcrum: A Post-Mortem Analysis'.

213 Interviews with author.

214 Connelly, 'Indonesia's New North Natuna Sea: What's in a Name?'.

215 Liza Yosephine, 'Indonesia Urges Parties to Respect Laws Following South China Sea Ruling', *Jakarta Post*, 12 July 2016, https://www.thejakartapost.com/seasia/2016/07/12/indonesia-urges-parties-to-respect-laws-following-south-china-sea-ruling.html.

216 Interview with author.

217 ASEAN Outlook on the Indo–Pacific, https://asean.org/storage/2019/06/ASEAN-Outlook-on-the-Indo-Pacific_FINAL_22062019.pdf.

218 Interviews with author.

219 Interviews by author with Indonesian and foreign diplomats.

220 Julie Hirschfeld Davis, 'President Joko Widodo of Indonesia Joins Trans-Pacific Partnership', *The New York Times*, 26 October 2015, https://www.nytimes.com/2015/10/27/us/politics/president-joko-widodo-of-indonesia-joins-trans-pacific-partnership.html.

221 Opening Statement by President Joko Widodo at the Asian–African Conference, 22 April 2015, http://www.bandungspirit.org/IMG/pdf/jokowi-jakarta_opening_statement-220415-bsn.pdf.

222 'Ambassador Mahendra Siregar Appointed as Foreign Affairs Deputy', *Tempo*, 25 October 2019, https://en.tempo.co/read/1264284/ambassador-mahendra-siregar-appointed-as-foreign-affairs-deputy.

223 'Reinvigorating Investment', *Jakarta Post*, 29 October 2019, https://www.thejakartapost.com/academia/2019/10/29/reinvigorating-investment.html.

224 Wahyudi Soeriaatmadja, 'Jokowi to Meet Trump in US in March, Says Minister', *The Straits Times*, 26 February 2020, https://www.straitstimes.com/asia/se-asia/jokowi-to-meet-trump-in-us-in-march-says-minister.

225 'President Jokowi Urges Ambassadors to Boost Economic Diplomacy', Antara News, 10 January 2020, https://en.antaranews.com/news/139456/president-jokowi-urges-ambassadors-to-boost-economic-diplomacy.

226 Marchio Irfan Gorbiano, 'Tony Blair Joins SoftBank, UAE Crown Prince as Advisors for Indonesia's New Capital', *Jakarta Post*, 16 January 2020, https://www.thejakartapost.com/news/2020/01/16/from-uk-to-japan-govt-announces-foreign-interest-in-developing-new-capital-city.html.

227 Ceri Parker, 'Indonesia's President Says He is an Avenger Superhero Fighting Trade Wars', *World Economic Forum*, 12 September 2018, https://www.weforum.org/agenda/2018/09/thanos-wont-win-says-avenger-joko-widodo/.

228 For more on how the foreign ministry became increasingly activist under Wirajuda, see Greta Nabbs-Keller, 'Reforming Indonesia's Foreign Ministry: Ideas, Organization and Leadership', *Contemporary Southeast Asia* 35, No 1 (2013), 56–82, https://research-repository.griffith.edu.au/bitstream/

handle/10072/55369/86143_1.pdf;jsessionid=13BDA7CD5
4F2137197E3F2B1D0278A32?sequence=1.

229 Dave McRae, *More Talk than Walk: Indonesia as a Foreign Policy Actor*, Lowy Institute Analysis (Sydney: Lowy Institute for International Policy, 27 February 2014), https://www.lowyinstitute.org/publications/more-talk-walk-indonesia-foreign-policy-actor.

230 Dewi Fortuna Anwar, 'Indonesia–China Relations: To Be Handled With Care', *ISEAS Perspective Issue 2019*, No 19, 28 March 2019, https://www.iseas.edu.sg/images/pdf/ISEAS_Perspective_2019_19.pdf.

231 Gabe Lipton and Gabriella Turrisi, 'Graphic Truth: Indonesia's Mr. Popular', *GZero Media*, 16 April 2019, https://www.gzeromedia.com/graphic-truth-indonesias-mr-popular.

232 Nicolo Machiavelli, *The Prince* (Project Gutenberg e-book, 2006), http://www.gutenberg.org/files/1232/1232-h/1232-h.htm.

233 Benedict Anderson, *Language and Power: Exploring Political Cultures in Indonesia*, 28.

234 Aspinall, et al, 'Elites, Masses, and Democratic Decline in Indonesia'.

235 For an early example, see J. A. Verdoorn, 'Indonesia at the Crossroads', *Pacific Affairs* 19, No 4 (1946), 339–350.

236 'Is Indonesia at a Crossroads?', *The Economist*, 23 September 2013, https://www.economist.com/the-economist-explains/2013/09/22/is-indonesia-at-a-crossroads.

237 Ariel Heryanto, *Language of Development and Development of Language: The Case of Indonesia* (Canberra: Australian National University, 1995), 14, https://openresearch-repository.anu.edu.au/bitstream/1885/145809/1/PL-D86.pdf.

Acknowledgements

I want to thank Dr Michael Fullilove, the Executive Director of the Lowy Institute, and Alex Oliver, the Director of Research, for giving me the opportunity to join the Institute and the backing to pursue important projects like this.

Sam Roggeveen helped frame and shepherd this book, as well as the wider Lowy Institute Paper series, and Sandra Rigby and Clare Caldwell provided invaluable editing support. Two anonymous external reviewers offered important critical insights that have undoubtedly improved my text.

There are dozens more people without whose assistance I could not have written this book. Many of them are in Indonesia, and they would prefer to go nameless, for obvious reasons. I am forever grateful to them and hope that my efforts are worthy of the time they took to explain their country to me.

A researcher is only as good as their sources.

Lowy Institute Papers

LOWY INSTITUTE PENGUIN SPECIALS

1. *Beyond the Boom*, John Edwards (2014)

2. *The Adolescent Country*, Peter Hartcher (2014)

3. *Condemned to Crisis*, Ken Ward (2015)

4. *The Embarrassed Colonialist*, Sean Dorney (2016)

5. *Fighting with America*, James Curran (2016)

6. *A Wary Embrace*, Bobo Lo (2017)

7. *Choosing Openness*, Andrew Leigh (2017)

8. *Remaking the Middle East*, Anthony Bubalo (2018)

9. *America vs The West*, Kori Schake (2018)

10. *Xi Jinping: The Backlash*, Richard McGregor (2019)

11. *Our Very Own Brexit*, Sam Roggeveen (2019)

Discover a
new favourite